SKETCHBOOK ON THE WORLD

John Giddens
All my best to a fellow
architect and Eagle Scout.
Terrance J. Brown, FAIA

SKETCHBOOK
ON THE WORLD

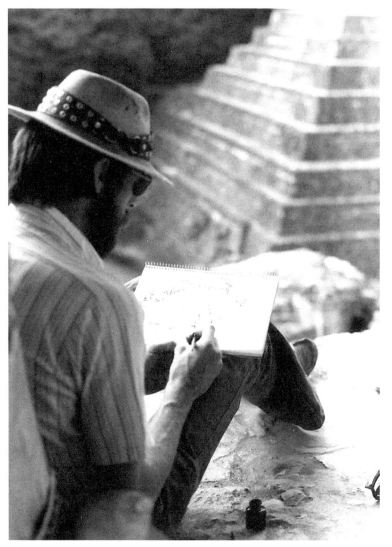

The author sketching Mayan Temple of the Inscriptions.
Palenque, Mexico, 1981.

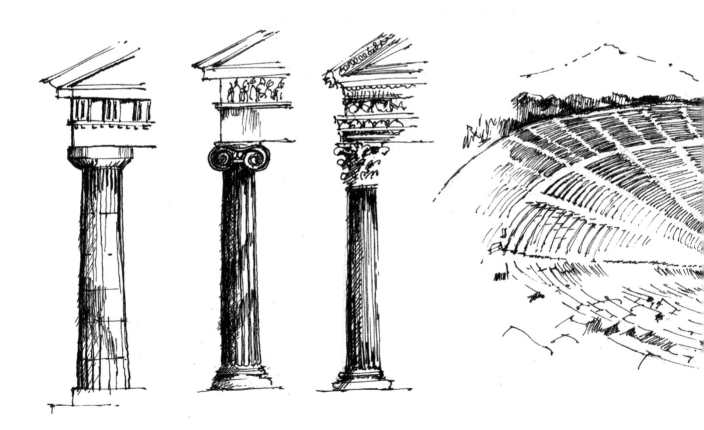

SKETCHBOOK ON THE WORLD

Pen and Ink Travel Sketches

Terrance J. Brown, FAIA

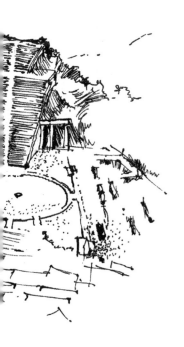

SUNSTONE PRESS

SANTA FE

Sunstone books may be purchased for educational, business, or sales promotional use.
For information please write: Special Markets Department, Sunstone Press,
P.O. Box 2321, Santa Fe, New Mexico 87504-2321.
Printed on acid-free paper

Library of Congress Cataloging-in-Publication Data

Names: Brown, Terrance J., 1945- author.
Title: Sketchbook on the world : pen and ink travel sketches / by Terrance J.
   Brown, FAIA.
Description: Santa Fe : Sunstone Press, 2017.
Identifiers: LCCN 2017036272| ISBN 9781632932044 (softcover : alk. paper) |
   Subjects: LCSH: Brown, Terrance J., 1945---Travel. | Brown,
   Terrance--Notebooks, sketchbooks, etc.
Classification: LCC NA737.B698 A2 2017 | DDC 720.92--dc23
LC record available at https://lccn.loc.gov/2017036272

The following drawings were published by John Wiley & Sons, Inc. in Drawing Shortcuts by Jim Leggitt, FAIA, 2nd
edition, 2010, ISBN 978-0-470-43548-9 (pbk.): "The Alamo" (Pg. 17) and "Chicago" (Pg. 17).

The following drawings were published by McGraw-Hill in Building Security by Barbara A. Nadel, FAIA, 2004,
ISBN 0-07-141171-2: "Pennsylvania Avenue" (Pg. 1.7), "Independence Hall" (Pg. 1.17), "Renaissance Vinoy Resort"
(Pg. 1.18), "The Castle" (Pg. 1.24), "Rachofsky House" (Pg. 1.36), "Kimball Art Museum" (Pg. 15.2).

The following drawings were previously published by Arte y Ciencia, S.A. in Antigua, Guatemala City and Area Guide,
1979: "Arco de Santa Catalina and Volcan Agua" (Cover), "La Merced Church Courtyard Fountain" (Pg. 7), "Column Detail"
(Pg. 17), "Santa Clara Cloister Courtyard Fountain" (Pg. 20), "Antigua Guatemala and Volcano"
(Pg. 26), "Carved Stone Entry" (Pg. 29), "Corner Window Balcony" (Pg.42), and "Bronze Door Knocker" (Pg. 57).

SUNSTONE PRESS IS COMMITTED TO MINIMIZING OUR ENVIRONMENTAL IMPACT ON THE PLANET. THE PAPER USED IN THIS BOOK IS FROM RESPONSIBLY MANAGED FORESTS. OUR PRINTER HAS
RECEIVED CHAIN OF CUSTODY (COC) CERTIFICATION FROM: THE FOREST STEWARDSHIP COUNCIL™ (FSC®), PROGRAMME FOR THE ENDORSEMENT OF FOREST CERTIFICATION™ (PEFC™), AND THE
SUSTAINABLE FORESTRY INITIATIVE® (SFI®). THE FSC® COUNCIL IS A NON-PROFIT ORGANIZATION, PROMOTING THE ENVIRONMENTALLY APPROPRIATE, SOCIALLY BENEFICIAL AND
ECONOMICALLY VIABLE MANAGEMENT OF THE WORLD'S FORESTS. FSC® CERTIFICATION IS RECOGNIZED INTERNATIONALLY AS A
RIGOROUS ENVIRONMENTAL AND SOCIAL STANDARD FOR RESPONSIBLE FOREST MANAGEMENT.

WWW.SUNSTONEPRESS.COM

SUNSTONE PRESS / POST OFFICE BOX 2321 / SANTA FE, NM 87504-2321 /USA
(505) 988-4418 / ORDERS ONLY (800) 243-5644 / FAX (505) 988-1025

*To my wife Sandra
and my twin brother
Morris Brown, FAIA*

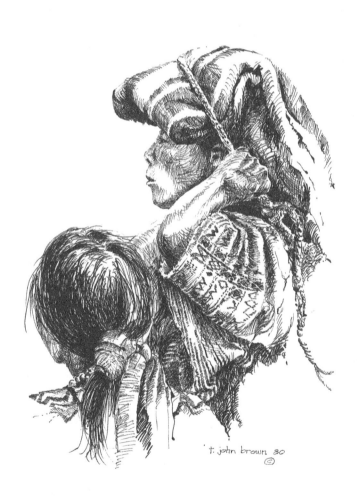

t. john brown 80
©

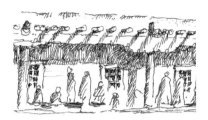

156

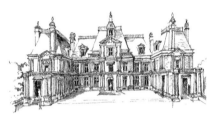

32

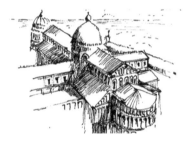

43

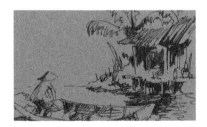

51

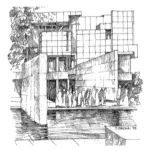

169

TABLE OF C

ONTENTS

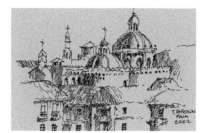

81

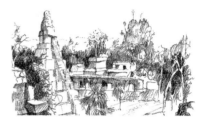

93

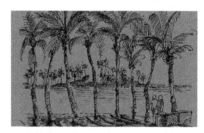

115

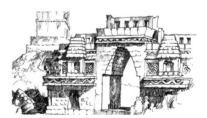

109

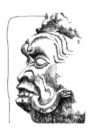

101

Preface

Preface

This book is much more than just another drawing book. It shares stories and pen and ink drawings of hundreds of scenes from my journeys. This book is arranged by countries and states and I urge you to open the book at any page and begin exploring. The drawings in the section titled Europe are my earliest works and were sketched when I was a college student. Many people including architecture students, designers, and even architects themselves, have limited freehand drawing ability for which the invention of computer drawing has played a part. I hope that this book inspires people interested in freehand drawing to use this book as a guide. There is no time like the present to begin drawing the world around you. The simple act of drawing will change how you see the world.

My drawings are typically sketched outdoors and often in a hurry. I usually begin with light pencil lines to ensure proportions are correct and that the scene will fit the page. Sometimes I begin a drawing and complete it later. Drawing when you are sightseeing with friends or family is a challenge because most folks don't want to hang around while you sketch. Thus, you learn to draw fast and loose, which in many cases, is a good thing for your drawing. Drawings are my souvenirs. They each have a story and often take the place of photographs. However, it might be useful to take a photo of a scene you are drawing so you can reference it if you need to complete your drawing later.

A drawing requires the artist to interpret what is being observed: a window detail or the items you see in a museum exhibit, the museum building itself or the people in it. A drawing can be done as you watch people waiting to board a plane or while you visit places you have never been before. It can be performed with many different tools such as pen and ink, pencil, colored pencil or even a brush which is skillfully used in Japanese ink wash paintings. Objects such as sticks, the thin edge of a sliced potato, and feathers dipped in any color of ink can also be used as drawing tools. Antoine Predock, FAIA, American Institute of Architects Gold Medal recipient, made many skillful drawings with found objects during his early years touring Europe. The act of drawing indelibly fixes the scene in your mind.

For the beginner, drawing can be difficult. As you develop your skill and confidence, the process becomes easier and certainly more enjoyable. I encourage you to begin by drawing simple objects to avoid being overwhelmed. Don't be afraid to take a drawing class. As your skill improves and you learn the basics of shade and shadow, single point and two-point perspective, the act of drawing will feel more comfortable. Practice until your drawing, made with simple lines, dashes and dots, resemble the item or scene you are looking at. Drawing should be fun but if you want to improve; practice, practice, practice.

Because I am an architect, I am naturally fascinated by the built environment and my drawings reflect this. Many of the human figures in these drawings are imprecisely drawn in terms of facial features and physical details, hands, etc. I place people in the drawings to provide a human quality and scale to the drawing. Ink drawings will not smudge and they provide excellent copies with a standard home printer. My early work was done with a crow quill pen and India ink. I prefer the varied line

weights that these flexible metal pen points provide, but for practicality, I now draw with a 0.5 to 0.7 mm roller ball Micro pen with black ink. Sketchbooks come in a variety of sizes and are available in many book stores. I typically carry an 8 1/2 x 11 inch hardback book with acid free paper (a must to preserve your work). A shoulder bag to carry your sketch book along with several pens, pencils and an eraser should be an essential part of your drawing equipment. You should carry extra pens for emergencies. I always place my sketch book in two durable plastic bags for protection. I have experienced various unexpected near disasters, where if my sketchbook was not protected, would have been damaged by water or spilled coffee.

The Beginning

Drawing came easy for me and I excelled in high school art classes, where I learned to work with various mediums to include tempera, water color, pencil, and colored pencil drawings. These skills helped me decide to become an architect. However, it wasn't until I took a pen and ink drawing class from Professor Dudley Thompson and history of architecture classes from Professor Nolan Barrick, FAIA, at Texas Tech University that the allure of pen and ink drawing captured my attention and provided me with the perfect instrument to record my travels. I learned how to use the flexible nibs of the crow quill pen to vary line weight for different effects. My first pen and ink drawing was done in 1965 from the third floor of the architecture building looking over the rooftop of the campus utility plant towards the tall lights of the football stadium at Texas Tech. The arch in this drawing is emblematic of the campus Spanish Renaissance architectural style.

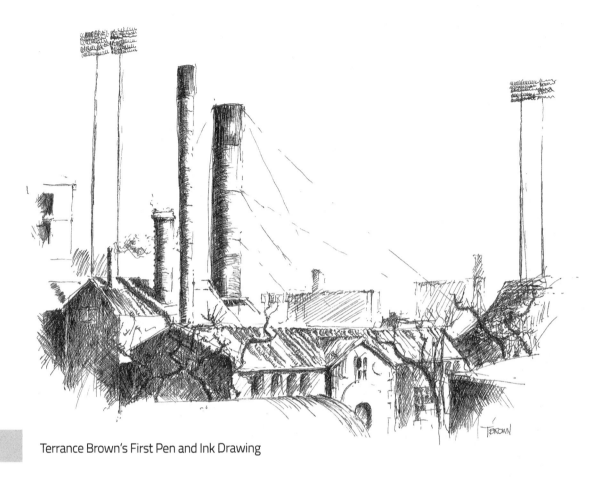

Terrance Brown's First Pen and Ink Drawing

Professor Barrick required us to fill sketchbooks with pen and ink drawings of historic buildings and details from various sources to help us learn their importance to the history of architecture. Many of these historic buildings were drawn quite small with very fine pen points which enabled me to capture distinctive details. I was influenced by the architectural drawings in books titled *History of Architecture* by Sir Banister Fletcher and *Guide to Western Architecture* by John Gloag. The book titled *Rendering in Pen and Ink* by Arthur L. Guptill has been my drawing guide and a general "how to" for drawing details with pen and ink.

Europe

My identical twin brother, Morris Brown, FAIA, and I grew up in the small town of Hardin, Montana, a remote western community beside the Crow Indian Reservation. The farthest we had ever been from home was in 1962 when our father drove our family to Renton, Washington to visit our uncle then down the Pacific coast to Disneyland. Studying ancient European architecture in college opened our eyes to a much larger world filled with buildings older than anything we had ever seen. The fascination of traveling in Europe became paramount after our study of architectural history at the Texas Tech University School of Architecture. We were introduced to a comprehensive analysis of Prehistoric, Egyptian, West Asiatic, Greek, and Roman architecture. That was followed with Early Christian, Byzantine, Romanesque, and Gothic architecture. The next semester we studied a comparison of typical palace facades of Florence and Venice Italy then moved on to Renaissance Italian and French Château and early and late Renaissance Houses of England.

The seminal moment I began to carry a sketch book was in 1966 with my brother, traveling across Europe during our third summer break from college. We compiled a list of historic buildings we had studied in our architectural history classes and squeezed, along with our backpacks, in a Texas Tech's professor's Volkswagen "beetle" and drove to New York City. The trip took three days and we slept on the ground alongside the highway. In New York City, Morris and I checked into an inexpensive YMCA hotel in Manhattan and slept head to foot on a single bed. We spent a few days walking around exploring and sketching scenes such as the Empire State Building, The Frick Collection (an art museum) and the Guggenheim Museum by Frank Lloyd Wright.

We flew to London, England and found out the World Cup soccer tournament was in full swing causing difficulty finding a place to stay. We located a gymnasium with young people from all over Europe sleeping on the floor and stage. In southern England on a rainy night the only place we could find to sleep was on the floor of a public toilet in a park. After a few days exploring London, we hitchhiked to Nottingham where we stayed with a childhood friend and his family. His father helped us find jobs for two weeks as laborers at the coal mine where he worked. We needed the income since we only had forty dollars apiece for expenses after paying for our air fare and train tickets. The coal mine work paid

us a hundred dollars apiece, which gave us a small financial cushion.

After exploring Paris and French country houses along the Loire River, we began a whirlwind tour of Europe via train for twenty-one days which took us to Spain, Italy, Germany, Austria, Denmark, Sweden, Belgium, Holland and Luxembourg. Several of the drawings from that trip were done with broad-tip pencil and are included in this book.

The art of drawing should be fun, but if you want to improve, practice, practice, practice.

Asia

graduated from Texas Tech in May of 1969 with a Bachelor of Architecture Degree and a Commission in the US Army as a Second Lieutenant and stayed in Lubbock, Texas to watch the momentous moon flight when Neil Armstrong was the first man to walk on the moon. Then I picked up my sketch book and took off to explore Europe again before entering active duty in the U.S. Army. This time I landed in

Luxembourg and began to hitchhike across Europe and found late summer to be cold and rainy. Many of the drawings I did were drawn with soft broad-tipped pencil and pen and ink.

At a Munich youth hostel, I spotted a guy placing a note on the bulletin board announcing he was searching for someone to help him drive his new Mercedes Benz to Kuwait. He told me he had little driving experience and already had a fender bender. I had never heard of Kuwait, but suspected it to be somewhere south of the Mediterranean and likely warmer than Europe so I volunteered to drive him. We slept in the car and traveled across Germany, Austria, and what used to be called Yugoslavia, and Bulgaria and crossed Turkey to Syria.

We parted ways at the Syrian border because the border guards were upset at the United States and would not let me cross into their country. My friend said the guards were mad because the United States recently sold military jets to Israel. I headed back to the coast and flew to Beirut, Lebanon for a student rate of ten dollars and hitchhiked down towards the Israeli border then to the ancient Roman ruins of Baalbek near the Lebanon border with Syria. I noted that people in Lebanon were uncomfortable seeing me hitchhiking and often paid a taxi driver to take me farther down the road or to my destination. Then I returned to Turkey and steamed along the Mediterranean coast of Turkey exploring coastal towns of Iskenderun, Adana, Mersin, Antalya, Marmaris and Kusadasi. There, I found a plane flight to Athens Greece for the same $10 student rate and spent several days exploring and sketching Athens and the ruins of the Acropolis. An Austrian youth named Frank and I took a long train ride, back to Vienna, sleeping on the luggage racks above the people below. From Vienna, I rushed back to Paris and flew home to Montana where I entered the Army.

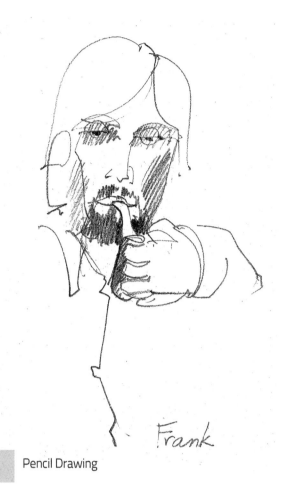

Pencil Drawing

Vietnam War

n 1969 after studying architecture and attending the Army Reserve Officer Training Corp (ROTC) program during college, I went on active duty for two years in the Army. I was stationed at Fort Belvoir, Virginia for a year teaching map reading to Officer Candidate Students and shortly before being shipped to Vietnam as a First Lieutenant, I bought two blank-hard-covered sketch books at the University of California Berkley book store to chronicle day by day events of the iconic war that history has shown to be the cultural upheaval of our generation and revealing the perils of life in war.

I was on leave for a week, staying with my girlfriend in Berkley and she drove me to Oakland for my departure flight. As we were waiting in the terminal, she suggested that I draw a picture of how I felt.

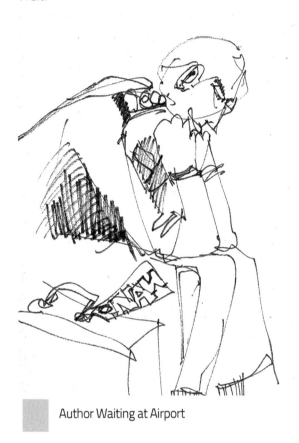

Author Waiting at Airport

When I arrived in Vietnam, the war had been raging for ten years and I was assigned to a small mapping unit. We traveled in Huey helicopters, sitting in the back seat beside the door gunners, gathering information and taking photos of jungle landing strips, bridges, port facilities, and remote artillery base construction.

I turned twenty-six in this far away country half way around the world. My pen and ink sketches, record army life, scenes of war, lush jungle, and villagers wearing conical shaped hats, all of which

gripped my senses. The drawings in the Vietnam section of this book illustrates life in war as I saw it.

Sri Lanka

I dedicated many years of my professional life helping people and communities recover from natural disasters. In early 2005, while serving as Chair of the American Institute of Architects (AIA) National Disaster Assistance Committee, I was asked by the President of the AIA to lead a team of professionals to the island of Sri Lanka off the southern coast of India, to observe and study the damage to the homes and coastal landscape. The U.S. Agency for International Development estimated "between 31,000 to 37,000 people were killed and 100,000 homes were destroyed in Sri Lanka." As we traveled along the coastal area, we managed to tour a few of the country's inland historic sights before returning to the USA. We published a report detailing how Sri Lanka architects and engineers can better prepare their communities from future tsunami disasters. Several of my sketches are used to illustrate this document. The other drawing made during our travel help me remember the devastation and historic beauty of this island country.

Central and South America

After my service in the Vietnam War I decided to explore Latin America. I had already traveled across Europe twice so I wanted a new experience. I trekked from 1971 to 1973 by hitch hiking, bus, train, boat and airplane from Montana to the southern tip of South America, crossing every country in Central and South America except for three small remote countries, the Guyana's, and Venezuela. At first, I traveled with a college friend named Danelle Crowley across Mexico and the Guatemalan jungle to the magnificent Mayan ruins of Tikal. In Antigua, Guatemala I studied Spanish at the Proyecto Lingüístico Francisco Marroquín (PLFM) school for two months and learned enough Spanish to make my experience more enjoyable. Danelle stayed in Guatemala for a while longer to help a young Mayan woman who was ill and required help with her baby.

I toured Panama City and the Panama Canal then flew to Columbia and traveled by rickety old school buses along the steep and mostly gravel Andes Mountain roads across Columbia, Ecuador, Peru and Bolivia. I was fascinated with the Inca people and the mixed cultures in these countries. I sketched the Spanish Colonial churches and street scenes along the way and hiked across the Andes to explore the unique ruins of Machu Pichu.

After the long, bone jarring, stretch of traveling along the Andes from Colombia to Bolivia I decided to settle down and find a job in Buenos Aires, Argentina. I worked for one of South America's most famous architects, Clorindo Testa, for three months. About that time, Danelle, made it to Buenos Aires and we traveled together to Chile, then by boat south along the Chilean Coast to the Straights of Magellan and on to the island of Tierra del Fuego. We traveled as far as the road in South America could take us.

Then we hitchhiked back to Buenos Aires, and I traveled by myself to Rio de Janeiro, Brazil where I bought a plane ticket with the remainder of my money to Mexico. I figured I could hitchhike from Mexico City to Texas for the fifty dollars I had left in my pocket.

I landed in Guatemala to visit my friends at the PLFM and the family I stayed with when I studied Spanish. Interestingly, the managers of the PLFM

Drawing requires the artist to interpret what they are observing in a new way.

The act of drawing will change the way you see the world around you.

just signed a contract to train U.S. Peace Corp Volunteers and hired me for a whopping twenty-five dollars a month to set up two training centers in the mountains. I got married in Guatemala, had two daughters, and lived there for eight years.

After those years of traveling and living in Latin America, my family and I settled in El Paso, Texas for six years where I completed my architecture internship and received a New Mexico license to practice architecture. Then we moved to Albuquerque, New Mexico, where I forged an award winning architectural career. As a specialist in international affairs I was selected by the American Institute of Architects (AIA) President Ron Skaggs, FAIA, to serve as a AIA Ambassador to the board of directors of the Federation of Pan American Architect Associations from 2001 to 2007. During that same time, I also served on the AIA International Committee and flew to Brazil, Ecuador, Colombia, Costa Rica, Honduras, Mexico, Panama and the Caribbean Islands of Puerto Rico and Guadalupe. This time, I traveled more like a diplomat and stayed in better hotels. I did not want to miss anything during these travels and continued to draw in my sketch book at every opportunity during these new visits to Latin American cities. By this time, I was sketching exclusively with a black Micro ball pen for its convenience.

Caribbean

During my travels with the Federation of Pan American Architect Associations (FPAA), I had the opportunity to travel to Puerto Rico various times, and the West Indies Island of Guadeloupe. Years earlier, when I lived in Guatemala, I was contacted to provide a hurricane damage assessment of every public building on the Island of St. Lucia. I traveled to Barbados where I met my disaster expert friends and did an extensive evaluation and sketched the damage of each public building for our report.

The island of Guadeloupe is a beautiful French island where the trade winds help cool the island. The currency is the Euro, so it was difficult to get used to how expensive everything was. I sat in international meetings all day with limited time to draw but managed to squeeze in several quick drawings at the hotel and faces of people attending the meeting.

The old Spanish Colonial El Moro Fort in Puerto Rico is a fascinating national monument and I spent a day there exploring Old Town and sketching various views of this Colonial relic that pirates frequently attacked.

North America

While serving as Chair of the AIA National Disaster Assistance Committee, I had the opportunity to travel to various Canadian Provinces where I trained architects to work after disasters.

Circumstances sometimes required me to do a drawing out of my hotel window. That was the case in New Jersey where I chose to draw all the cars in the hotel parking lot from my twelfth floor room window. It was cold and wintery and I spent all day teaching a seminar so the parking lot was my record of that city.

I did not have any drawings of my home town, Hardin, Montana, so on a recent trip, I sketched an iconic turn of the century hotel across the street from the historic train station. Now I feel complete. Then I made a drawing at the nearby Battle of the Little Big Horn National Monument where the Civil War hero and Brevet General, George Custer, was killed along with all of the men in his command. Custer made a brash move to attack a much larger force of Sioux and Cheyenne warriors and was overwhelmed.

At the time of this book's publication, I don't hitchhike, and I have more money in my pocket than when I traveled as a young man but I continue to draw with pen and ink. I urge you to pick up a pen and illustrate how you view the world around you. I enjoy thumbing through my sketch books and reminisce about what was happening around me when I made these drawings. Each drawing has a story and bring back fond memories of my travels.

One of the travelers I met in Guatemala said, "travel adds dimension to the appreciation of home and an appreciation of where you've been when you return home." He is so right.

Acknowledgments

I owe a great deal of gratitude for the creativity, guidance, and support from my colleague and friend, Ed Vance, FAIA, principle and owner of EV&A Architects. Ed is a talented and creative architect, author and book designer and soon to be, Chancellor of the College of Fellows. He along with Kyle Fisher, Assoc. AIA, produced the original layout of this book over a four-year period. Ed's unrivaled support and encouragement for this book is remarkable.

My identical twin brother, Morris Brown, FAIA, MFA, a creative architect and gifted pen and ink artist, has been an inspiration to me all my life. He also carries a sketch book when he travels. I continuously looked over his shoulder when we traveled and sketched across Europe during college. His sketches are unrivaled and inspire me to keep up with him. Each time we get together we show each other our most recent drawings.

Rebecca Edmunds, a gifted writer and friend, edited the original manuscript. I am indebted to her for her concise editing and clear advice.

I am most grateful for a monetary gift from my friend and colleague Roy Hertweck, AIA, former President of the AIA Albuquerque and New Mexico Architectural Foundation, which helped with the publication of this book. His encouragement and support is greatly appreciated.

And I thank my publisher, James Clois Smith, Jr. at Sunstone Press for his guidance, concise editing skills and encouragement to publish this book.

EUROPE

When Morris and I arrived in London, our goal was to visit as many English manor houses as possible. During one of our trips we were driven by the father of the family we were staying with, to sketch an architectural masterpiece named Hardwick Hall in Derbyshire, built in 1597. We arrived after closing time and having come so far to see it, we impulsively climbed over the wall. To our surprise, our host climbed over the wall behind us. We walked around the grounds to get a better look but were eventually caught by guards and escorted off the site. That gave us a big laugh but I managed to get a quick sketch of the majestic building. The guards were not so hard on us college kids visiting from the USA, but told our host that being a respectable Englishman, he should have known better.

One of our side trips took us to Sherwood Forest of Robin Hood fame where we saw the age-old stately oak tree called Major Oak.

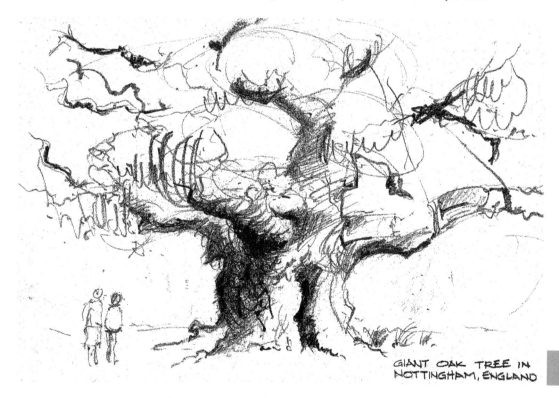

GIANT OAK TREE IN NOTTINGHAM, ENGLAND

This drawing was done with a soft broad-tipped pencil. Robin Hood is reputed to have hid out in the massive hollowed-out tree trunk which measures thirty-three feet in diameter. Later we hitchhiked south to the coast and skirted the massive prehistoric monument called Stonehenge. Because there did not seem to be much more to see than large stones standing-on-end in a circular manner, and since we had so much ahead of us to experience, we agreed to continue without stopping. It is estimated that this structure was built between 3,000 BC to 2,000 BC.

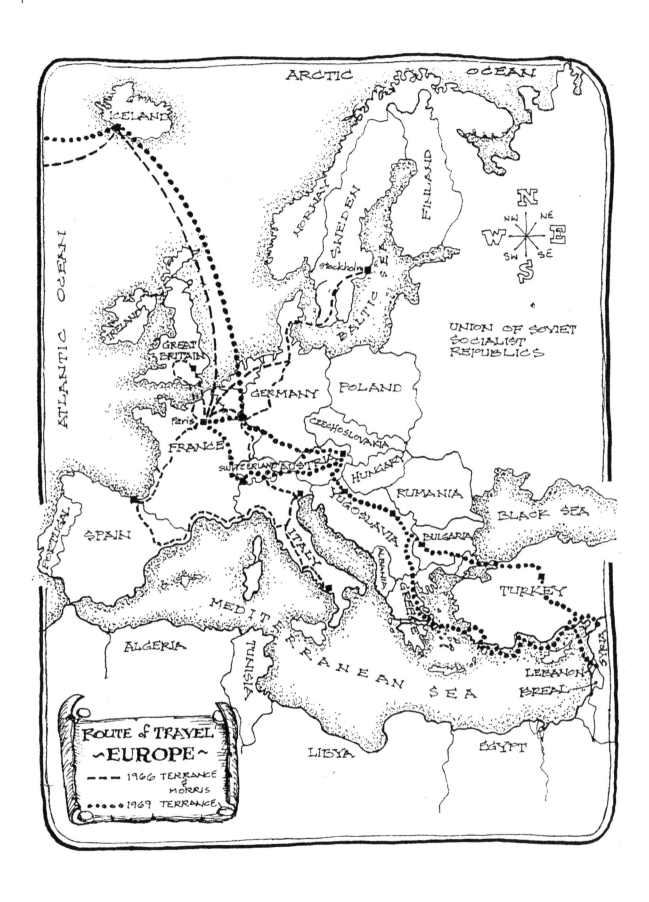

In Zaragoza, Spain we decided to start our railroad pass which ran consecutively for twenty-one days. We calculated that would take us across Europe and back to Paris with two days to spare before returning to New York. We traveled to Barcelona to explore the fluid Art Nouveau creations of the architect Antonio Gaudi. We couldn't speak Spanish, but when we asked directions in English, people pointed, assuming correctly, that we were looking for the great Sagrada Familia Cathedral that Gaudi designed. Little did Gaudi know that this building would take, in the European tradition of building cathedrals, a hundred years to complete. The cathedral is still being constructed.

Our next stop was Pisa, Italy to visit the Leaning Tower of Pisa. Our only regret was that it cost 25 cents to climb to the top of the tower and we decided to buy bread instead. My brother justified this saying that the tower could crumble while were climbing to the top. Then we traveled to Florence to visit Michelangelo's sculptures and Leonardo's paintings. Brunelleschi's transformative brick dome on the cathedral is one of the largest in Europe and is unlike anything ever built at that time. The stately Renaissance home of the Medici family and others appeared heavily rusticated with heavy stone walls on the lower portion of the buildings and minimal

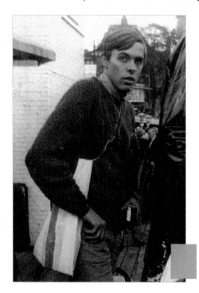

Terry Boarding a Boat in Amsterdam

ornament around the upper story windows, unlike the delicately designed homes we will see in Venice.

Rome was breathtaking. Exploring a city that is over a thousand years old was inconceivable for two Montana boys. The immense Vatican, Michelangelo's paintings in the Sistine Chapel, the Roman Forum, and Coliseum, and other architectural masterpieces were influential in building design around the world. Using Rome as a base, we traveled South to the ancient ruins of Pompeii, a sizeable Roman city that was smothered in ash from a volcanic eruption of Mt. Vesuvius in 79 AD. Then up to Venice, a city on water, to visit St. Mark's Cathedral on the Plaza with its multiple domes and the graceful and delicately detailed historic three and four story homes along the water's edge. In lieu of sidewalks, there were canals with poles sticking out of the water near the home's entrance to tie boats.

From Italy, we quickly traveled by train across Switzerland, Austria, Germany, Denmark, Belgium, and Holland and by ferry to Sweden, stopping at various cities in each of these countries and walking around for a day or two sketching scenes. Amsterdam, Holland was memorable due to people crowding the streets riding bicycles. The canals with boats plying the water added to the uniqueness of the city. One of the street photographers took a photo of me about to climb into a boat for a canal tour.

Back in Paris, we spent a couple days exploring sights not previously visited and happened to visit Notre Dame Cathedral during a church service. Music from the grand pipe-organ lifted our souls.

It was a wonderful trip and we completed many drawings. Morris and I frugally traveled on two dollars a day, unlike the popular guide book titled *Europe on Five Dollars a Day* but we lost about fifteen pounds apiece on our already lean bodies due to our meager diet and all the walking we did. Fortunately, the money earned working at the coal mine paid for our plane trip home from New York City, saving us from having to hitch hike across the country.

ENGLAND

My brother and I arrived in England eager to explore Hardwick Hall, so we naively climbed over the entry gate to have a closer look. A guard promptly escorted us off the property, but I still got the sketch.

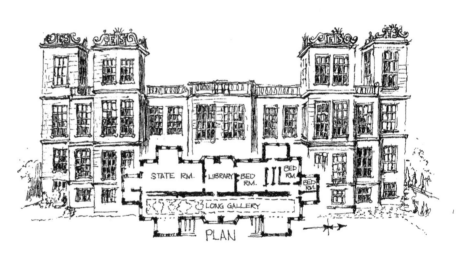

Harwick Hall
Derbyshire, England
Built 1576

The large country manor houses of the Elizabethan Period—the English Renaissance—were often built in a symmetrical "E" or "H" shape with a central entrance. However, that symmetry was not always enforced on the interior. Large expanses of window glazing were customary in houses of this period due to the invention of plate glass. During my visit to England, I worked for a week in a Nottingham coal mine to make a little money for my upcoming tour of Europe.

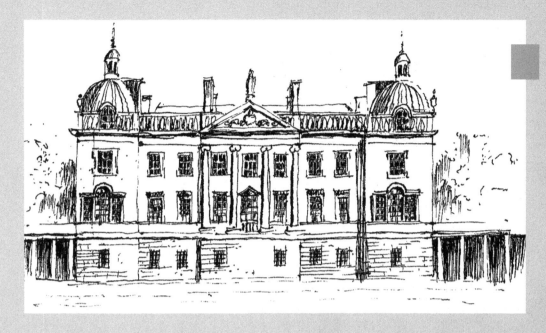

Houghton Hall
Norfolk, England
Built 1723

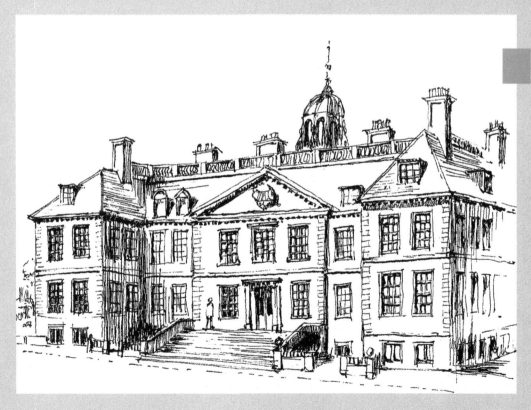

Belton House
Grantham, England
Built 1689

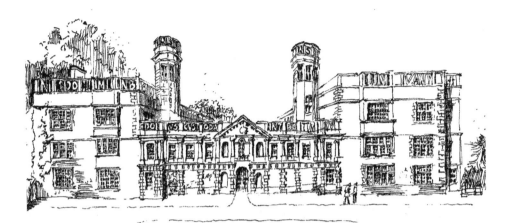

Castle Ashby
Northants, England
Built 1572

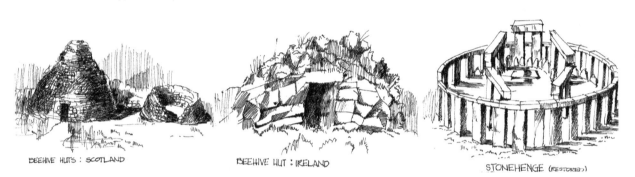

BEEHIVE HUTS : SCOTLAND

BEEHIVE HUT : IRELAND

STONEHENGE (RESTORED)

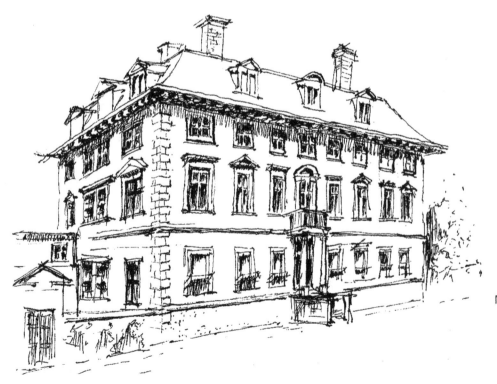

Thorpe Hall
Northants , England
Built 1656

" Every drawing tells a story.

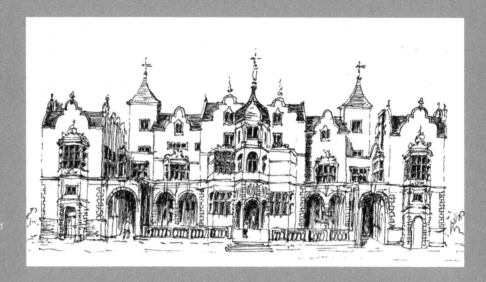

Holland House
Kensington, England
Built 1607

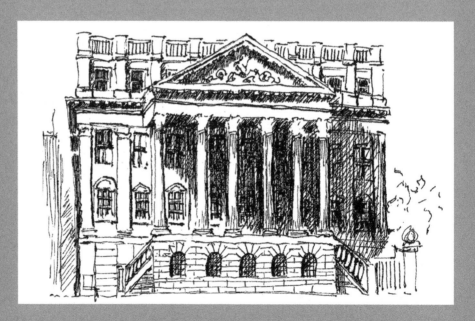

The Masion House
London, England
Built 1739-1757

FRANCE

Sketching 13th century soaring Gothic cathedral towers and flying buttresses helped me understand how meaningful and uplifting religion was to the early French people.

We hitchhiked to Salisbury, England to see the massive Salisbury Cathedral with England's tallest spire, built in 1228, then on to Brighton where we ferried across the English Channel to Dieppe, France. We arrived too late to find a youth hostel open, but we managed to find a farmer who let us sleep on fresh straw in his barn. Morris and I turned twenty years old that day.

In Paris, we sketched the magnificent Eiffel Tower named after it's designer, Gustave Eiffel. We climbed one of the towers of the Notre Dame Cathedral and sketched the tower's carved stone monster-like gargoyles which are considered protectors and are scary looking to ward off evil spirits.

Three days later, we hitchhiked to the exquisitely detailed Chartres Cathedral and the resplendent country palaces and gardens of Versailles and Fontainebleau. Then a guy from Mexico, driving a luxury French car called a Citroen, picked us up to keep him company while touring the impressive large country manor houses called château, along the Loire River, the longest river in France. Many of the beautiful structures we visited were built in the early 1500s. It was interesting to explore the French château after the English Manor houses. The large French houses had delicate detailing and unique shapes such as seen with the Château de Chenonceau, which was built over the Cher River. One thing of note is the smaller size of the French château windows which are not as expansive as the English Manor House windows built in the same period.

We were excited to visit gothic architecture, a style of building which flourished in Europe during the medieval period, characterized by the pointed arch, the ribbed-vault and the flying buttresses that supported the high cathedral walls. The cathedrals of Notre Dame and Chartres are powerful expressions of faith with ceilings "reaching to the sky," sculptural details of saints and large expanses of stained glass windows depicting biblical scenes.

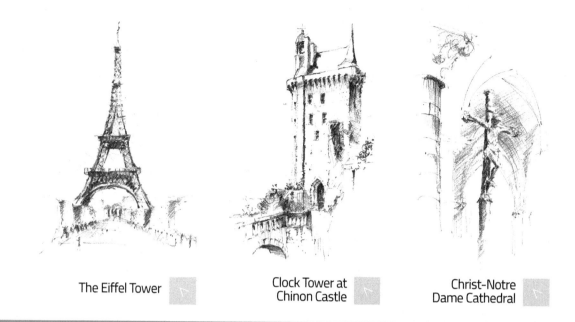

The Eiffel Tower

Clock Tower at
Chinon Castle

Christ-Notre
Dame Cathedral

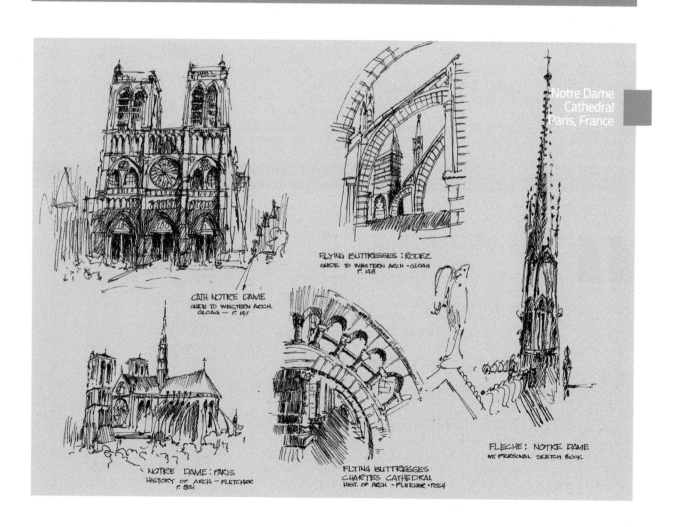

Notre Dame
Cathedral
Paris, France

FLYING BUTTRESSES : RODEZ
GUIDE TO WESTERN ARCH - GLOAG
P. 148

CATH NOTRE DAME
GUIDE TO WESTERN ARCH.
GLOAG – P. 147

NOTRE DAME : PARIS
HISTORY OF ARCH – FLETCHER
P. 551

FLYING BUTTRESSES
CHARTES CATHEDRAL
HIST. OF ARCH - FLETCHER - P.564

FLECHE : NOTRE DAME
MY PERSONAL SKETCH BOOK

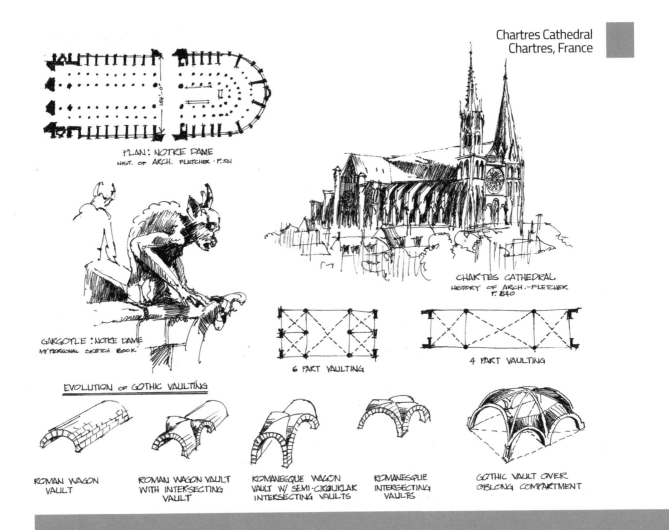

PLAN: NOTRE DAME
HIST. OF ARCH. FLETCHER · P. 581

Chartres Cathedral
Chartres, France

CHARTES CATHEDRAL
HISTORY OF ARCH.-FLETCHER
P. 540

GARGOYLE: NOTRE DAME
MY PERSONAL SKETCH BOOK

6 PART VAULTING

4 PART VAULTING

EVOLUTION of GOTHIC VAULTING

ROMAN WAGON VAULT

ROMAN WAGON VAULT WITH INTERSECTING VAULT

ROMANESQUE WAGON VAULT W/ SEMI-CIRCULAR INTERSECTING VAULTS

ROMANESQUE INTERSECTING VAULTS

GOTHIC VAULT OVER OBLONG COMPARTMENT

Plan on taking more time to draw these large buildings due to the great number of windows, elaborate roofs and intricate details.

Chateau D'Azay
Le Ridea
Built 1518-27

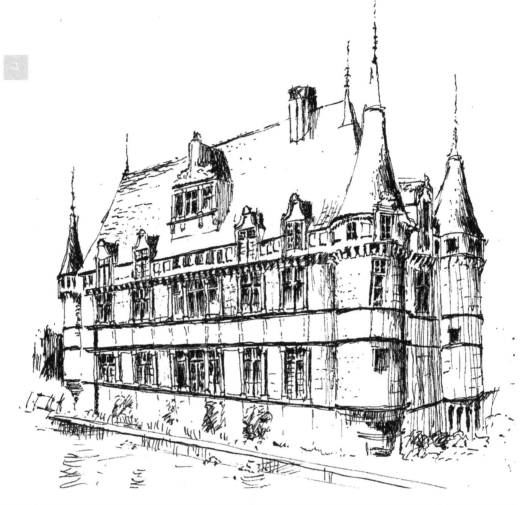

Chateau
De Chenonceau
Built 1515-23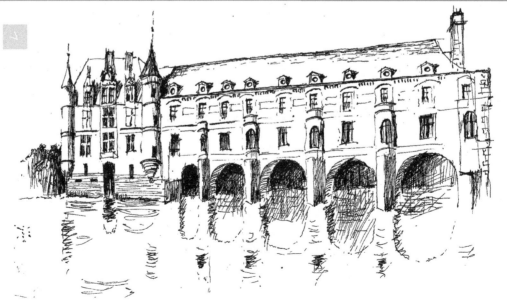

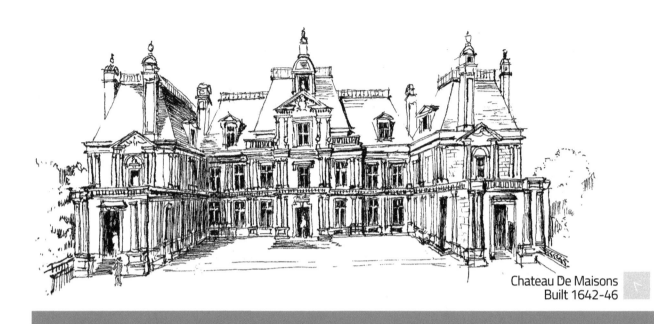

Chateau De Maisons
Built 1642-46

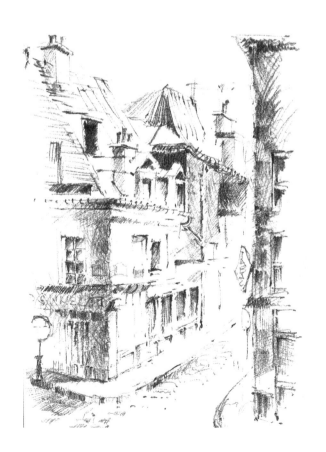

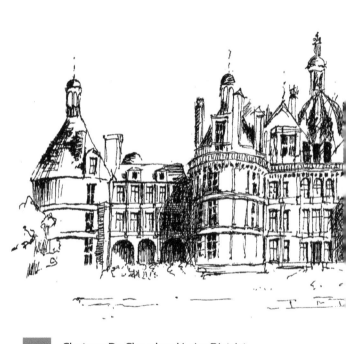

Chateau De Chambord Loire District
Built 1519-47

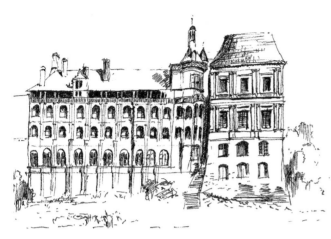

Chateau De Blois
on the River Loire

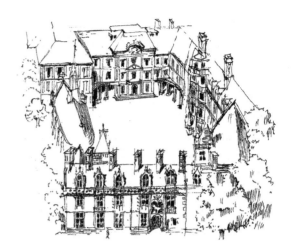

Chateau De Blois
Built 1498-1524

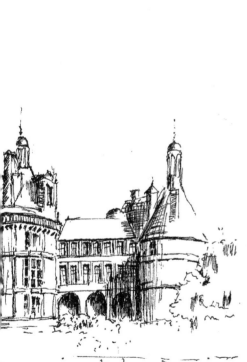

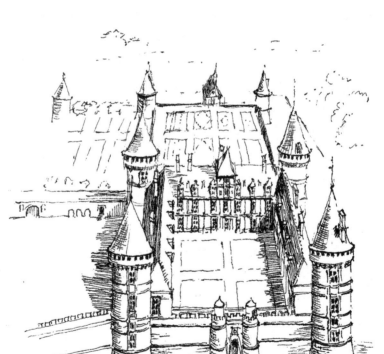

Chateau De Bury Near Blois
Built 1520

GREECE

The Doric column is the simplest of the three ancient Greek architectural orders. Many significant buildings around the world emulate the classical style of early Greek columns.

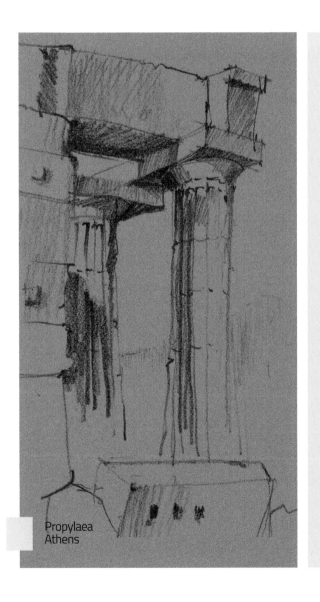

Propylaea
Athens

The drawings from Greece were done during a trip to Europe after I graduated from college. The day after arriving in Athens, a contractor building a four-story house came to the youth hostel looking for guys wanting to earn money. He had us carrying heavy tile to the roof deck. Thankfully, after learning that I was an architecture student, he asked me to supervise the work. I stayed in a Youth Hostel in Athens for several days and every evening I would run to the Acropolis to watch the sun go down while sitting on the steps of the Temple of Athena Nike. This small temple, built around 420 BC, sits beside the entrance to the Acropolis and is named after the Greek goddess, Athena.

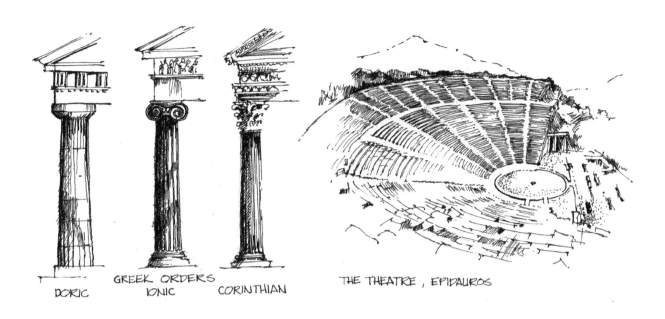

DORIC

GREEK ORDERS
IONIC

CORINTHIAN

THE THEATRE, EPIDAUROS

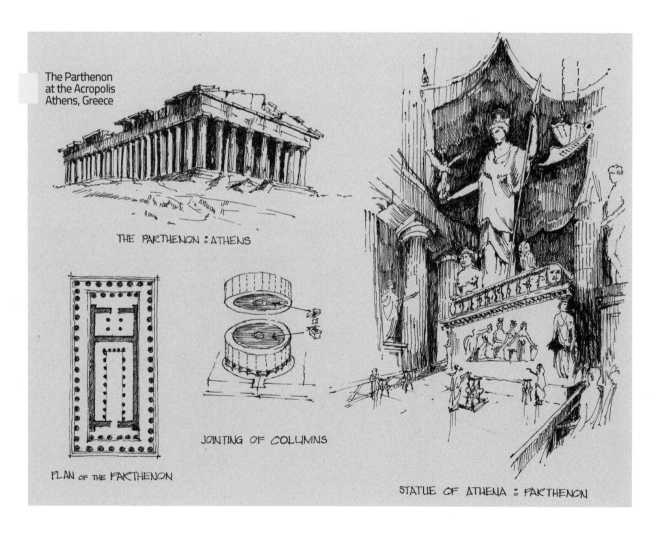

The Parthenon
at the Acropolis
Athens, Greece

THE PARTHENON : ATHENS

PLAN OF THE PARTHENON

JOINTING OF COLUMNS

STATUE OF ATHENA : PARTHENON

Column Detail
at the Parthenon

Sir Banister Fletcher's **A History of Architecture** notes that the finely crafted marble columns of classical Greek architecture are derived from earlier crafted wood columns.

The six delicate female figures called Caryatids (bottom of next page) support the roof of the Erechtheion temple on the Acropolis.

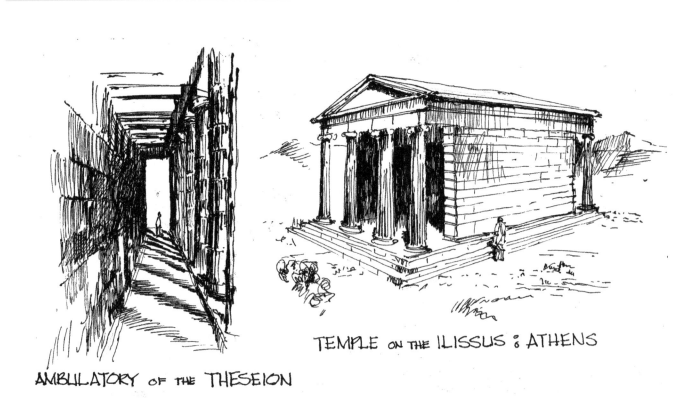

AMBULATORY of the THESEION

TEMPLE on the ILISSUS : ATHENS

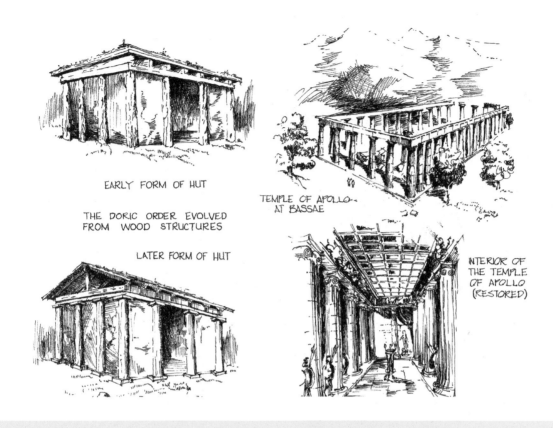

EARLY FORM OF HUT

THE DORIC ORDER EVOLVED
FROM WOOD STRUCTURES

LATER FORM OF HUT

TEMPLE OF APOLLO
AT BASSAE

INTERIOR OF
THE TEMPLE
OF APOLLO
(RESTORED)

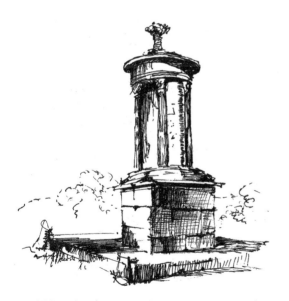

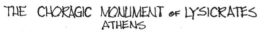

THE CHORAGIC MONUMENT OF LYSICRATES
ATHENS

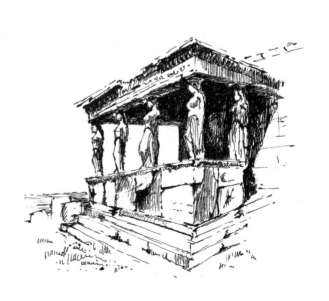

ITALY

My brother and I traveled and sketched our way across Italy in 1966. Our first stop was Rome and the Roman Forum at the city's heart. Traveling with another drawer often ensures plenty of time for sketching.

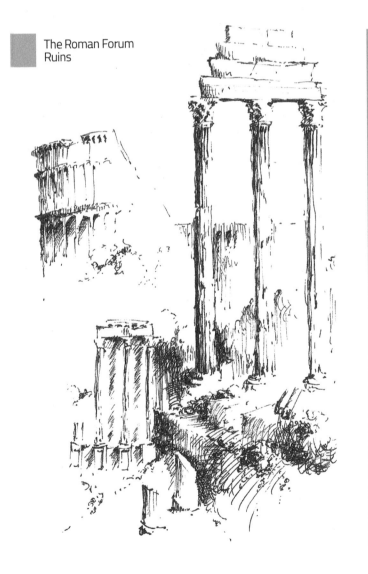

The Roman Forum
Ruins

Visiting Italy was a lifelong dream for a young architecture student, who could not get enough of the country's unique architecture. Italy is home to the Roman Forum and Coliseum, Venice's St. Mark's Cathedral and famous canals, and Michelangelo's sculptures in Florence. Each of these ancient cities has unique characteristics that offer great opportunities to sketch as you travel.

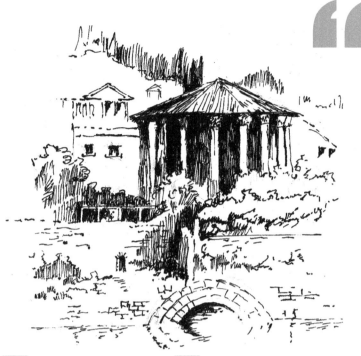

"

The drawing on the left illustrates Etruscan architecture in central Italy around 700 BC. The Etruscan people learned how to build large stone temples from the Greeks. The buildings below are Byzantine. The domes on St. Mark's Cathedral in Venice are particularly pronounced.

∧ Etruscan Cloaca

∨ St. Vitale and St. Mark's Cathedrals

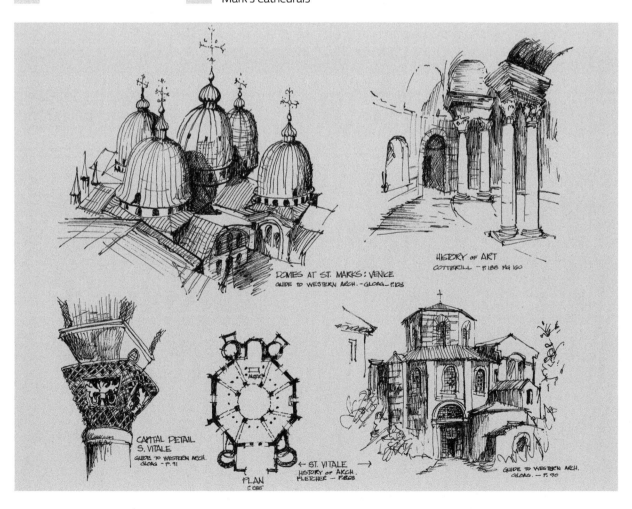

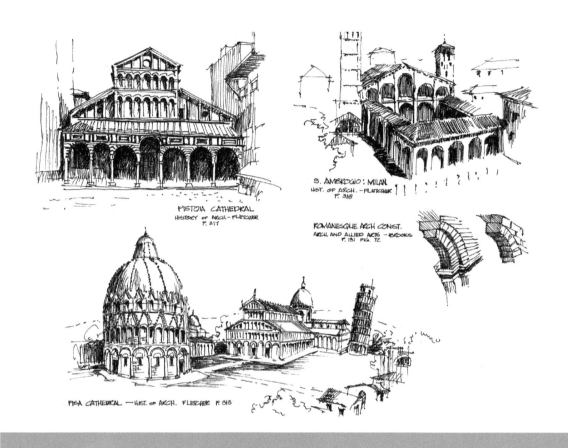

PISTOIA CATHEDRAL
HISTORY OF ARCH - FLETCHER
P. 317

S. AMBROGIO : MILAN
HIST. OF ARCH. - FLETCHER
P. 318

ROMANESQUE ARCH CONST.
ARCH AND ALLIED ARTS - BROOKS
P. 131 FIG. 72

PISA CATHEDRAL — HIST. OF ARCH. FLETCHER P. 313

The transition from rustic stone work on the ground floor to more delicate detailing on the upper stories makes Florence's Renaissance homes appear taller. The architecture of Venice is graceful and more decorative.

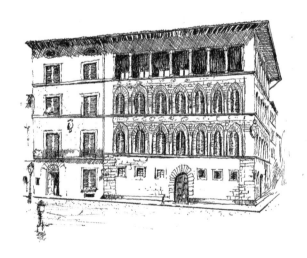

— PALAZZO GUADAGNI —
FLORENCE : AD. 1490

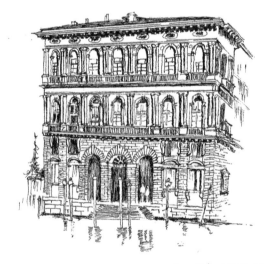

— PALAZZO CORNER DELLA CA' GRANDE —
VENICE : A.D. 1532

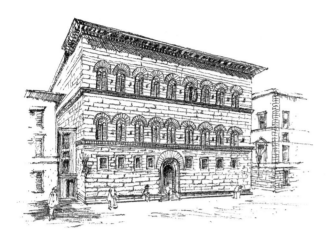

—PALAZZO STROZZI—
FLORENCE: A.D. 1489

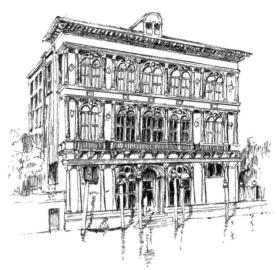

—PALAZZO VENDRAMINI—
VENICE: A.D. 1481

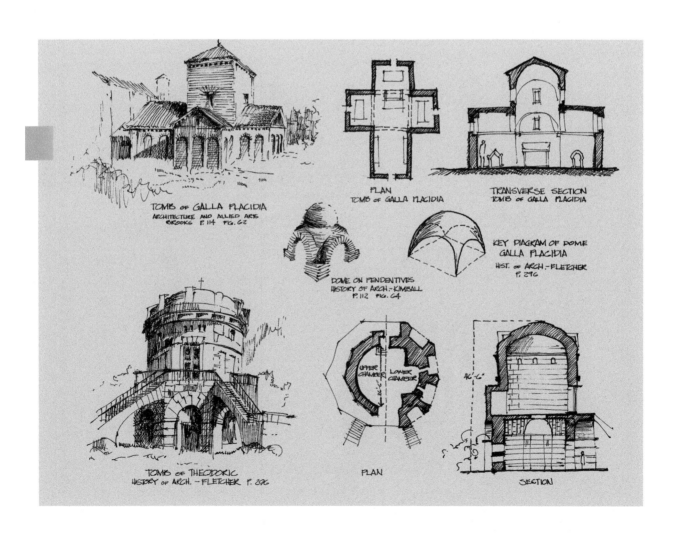

TOMB OF GALLA PLACIDIA
ARCHITECTURE AND ALLIED ARTS
BROOKS P. 114 FIG. 62

PLAN
TOMB OF GALLA PLACIDIA

TRANSVERSE SECTION
TOMB OF GALLA PLACIDIA

DOME ON PENDENTIVES
HISTORY OF ARCH. – KIMBALL
P. 112 FIG. 64

KEY DIAGRAM OF DOME
GALLA PLACIDIA
HIST. OF ARCH. – FLETCHER
P. 296

TOMB OF THEODORIC
HISTORY OF ARCH. – FLETCHER P. 296

PLAN
UPPER CHAMBER   LOWER CHAMBER

SECTION
46'-6"

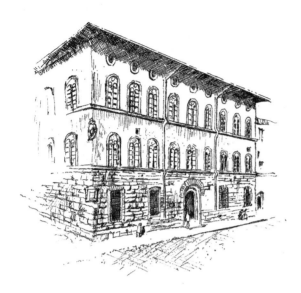

— PALAZZO QUARATESI —
FLORENCE : AD. 1445

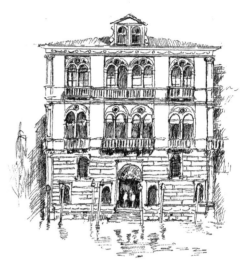

— PALAZZO CORNER SPINELLI —
VENICE : A.D. 1480

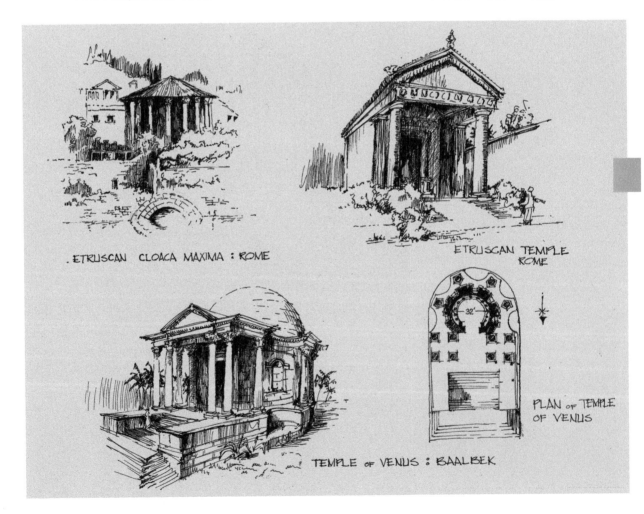

. ETRUSCAN CLOACA MAXIMA : ROME

ETRUSCAN TEMPLE
ROME

TEMPLE OF VENUS : BAALBEK

PLAN OF TEMPLE
OF VENUS

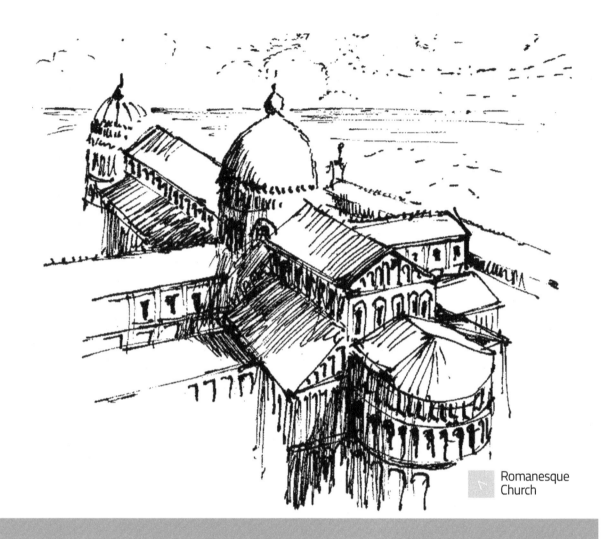

Romanesque
Church

The Roman
aqueducts, found
across Europe, are
engineering marvels
moving water
using gravity
alone to keep the
towns clean and free
from effluent.

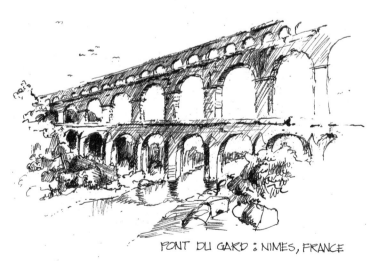

PONT DU GARD : NIMES, FRANCE

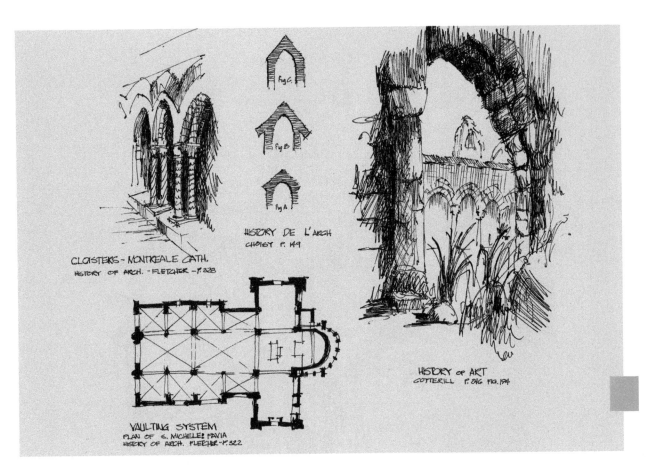

CLOISTERS - MONTREALE CATH.
HISTORY OF ARCH. - FLETCHER - P. 328

HISTORY DE L'ARCH
CHOISY P. 149

HISTORY OF ART
COTTERILL P. 246 FIG. 174

VAULTING SYSTEM
PLAN OF S. MICHELE: PAVIA
HISTORY OF ARCH. FLETCHER - P. 322

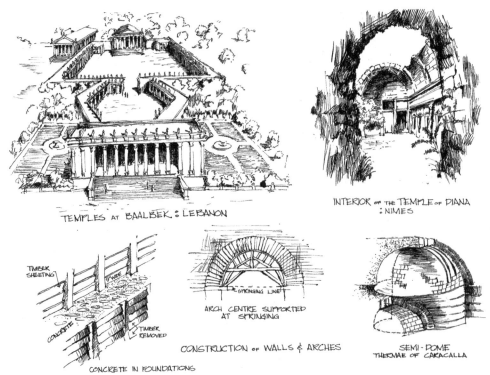

TEMPLES AT BAALBEK: LEBANON

INTERIOR OF THE TEMPLE OF DIANA
: NIMES

TIMBER SHEETING

CONCRETE IN FOUNDATIONS

ARCH CENTRE SUPPORTED
AT SPRINGING

CONSTRUCTION OF WALLS & ARCHES

SEMI - DOME
THERMAE OF CARACALLA

Ruins of Pompeii

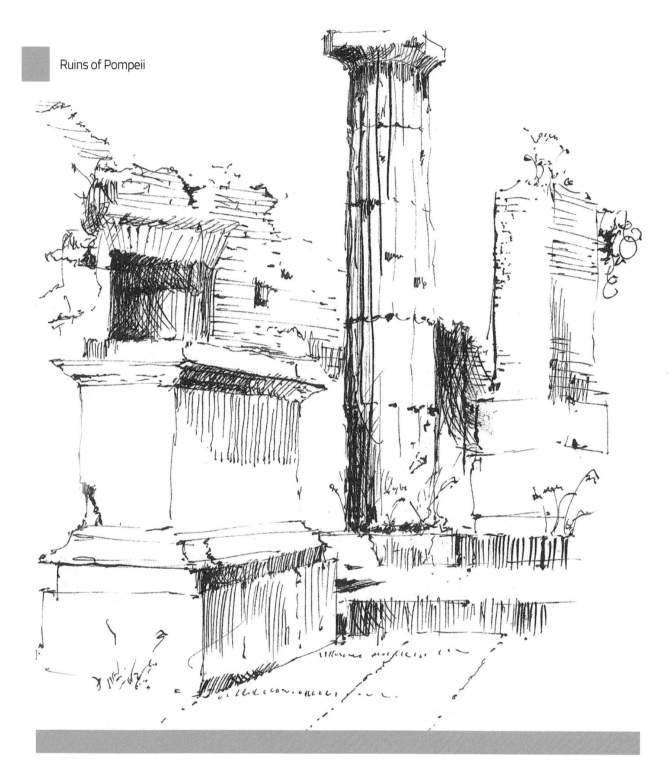

This is one of my first journal drawings (1966) made with pen and ink. A volcanic eruption of Mount Vesuvius in 79 AD buried ancient Pompeii under twenty feet of ash, leaving us the incredible experience of seeing an excavated, yet mostly intact, Roman village.

ASIA

The Vietnam war was the defining event of my generation. I was faced with the specter of this jungle war half way around the world from the time I graduated from high School in 1963 to 1969 when I graduated from college. If I had not been accepted in the university upon high school graduation, I would have been immediately drafted to serve in the war. Studying architecture delayed the inevitable for six years. By that time, I had a college degree and a Commission in the US Army Corp of Engineers as an Army officer thanks to the four-year Army ROTC Course that I was enrolled in. In 1971, after my first year in the Army I received orders to serve in Vietnam.

I arrived in Vietnam carrying a sketch book and I am thankful I had the forethought to record my life in that hot, steamy jungle war. When I arrived "in-country" I wanted to learn more about my far-away home and strangely, even during the height of this war, the military had organized a few sightseeing tours for soldiers and airman stationed around Saigon (now Ho Chi Minh City). We visited several churches and a Buddhist temple which fascinated me with the highly articulated colorful dragon guarding the entrance. Once inside, I found a cool, shaded open-air courtyard with giant spirals of incense hanging from roof beams. The sweet-smelling incense apparently stayed lit twenty-four hours a day.

The young Vietnamese women who worked on base usually wore the typical silk *Ao Dai* dresses, which flowed with the breeze and looked so refreshing to war-weary eyes.

I was stationed at a helicopter base called Plantation and lived in a wooden barracks with sandbag bunkers located between the buildings for protection. My mission was flying daily low level helicopter reconnaissance missions assessing road damage, bridge construction, trafficability of roads and feasibility of off-road movements. These Bell UH-1 Iroquois (nicknamed "Huey") helicopters were ubiquitous in this war for transporting soldiers and supplies and for medical evacuation. Normally we flew with the side doors open so the door gunners with their machine guns on a pivot were ready at-all-times. The drawing of the helicopter indicates a smaller heavily armed AH-1 Cobra attack helicopter providing support and protection for our work along the Cambodian border.

We also observed the massive D-8 Caterpillar bulldozers with mounted Rome Plows used by the Army to rip down jungle for land clearing operations. One of the caterpillar drivers told me that it was not uncommon to have screeching monkeys fall out the trees on them as they were knocking the jungle down.

One night when I was the officer in-charge of guard duty, I walked my rounds visiting each guard bunker in my section and caught a soldier smoking marijuana in the bunker called "Dublin Castle." I told him he was endangering everyone on the base and I would report him if I caught him smoking weed again. We crossed paths when he rotated off guard duty, and he thanked me for not reporting him.

We read books and played checkers and volleyball between helicopter flights. Oddly, one end of the volleyball court was alongside the protective coils of concertina wire which surrounded our base. It appears every game, someone would spike the ball into the wire, thus ending the play. We went through a lot of volley balls.

VIETNAM

Throughout my tour of duty in III Corps during the Vietnam War, I kept a journal. Drawing helped me cope with the war and better understand and appreciate the region's culture and its people.

Dragon Statue

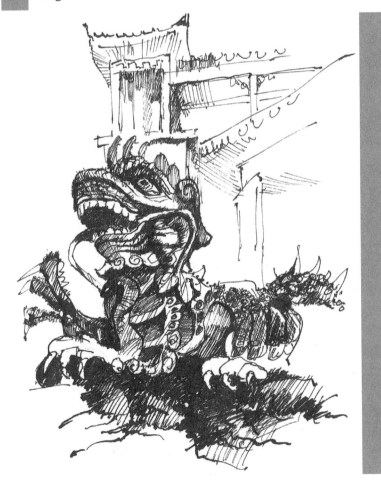

Military service members were offered guided tours of Saigon temples during the Vietnam War. This bold and iconic dragon stands guard at the first temple I visited shortly after arriving in Vietnam. The temple's interior courtyard was ringed with giant spirals of burning incense seen in the drawing on the next page. During my first helicopter flight, we flew to the top of a volcano-shaped mountain called Nui Ba Den, picked up a wounded soldier and flew him to a hospital. The flight around the mountain was as harrowing as it was thick with enemy soldiers.

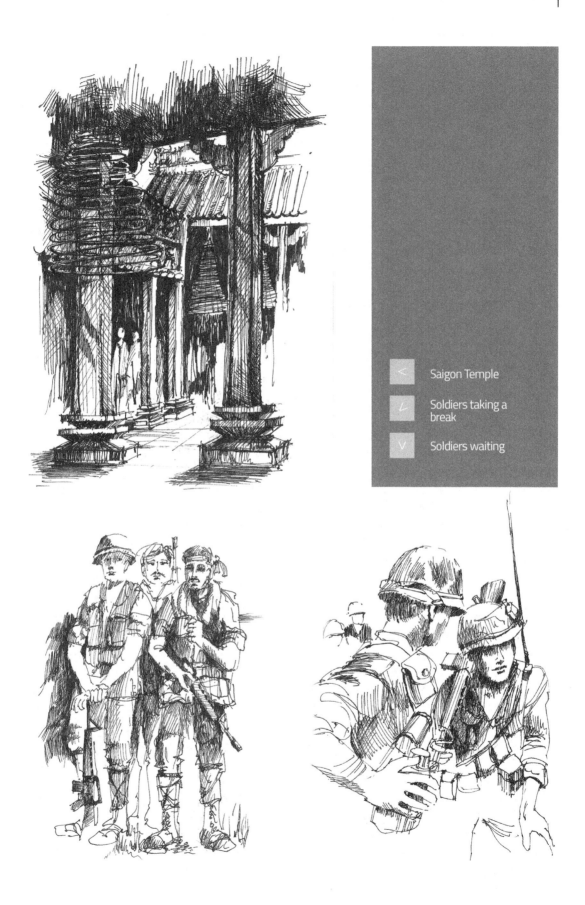

< Saigon Temple

∠ Soldiers taking a break

∨ Soldiers waiting

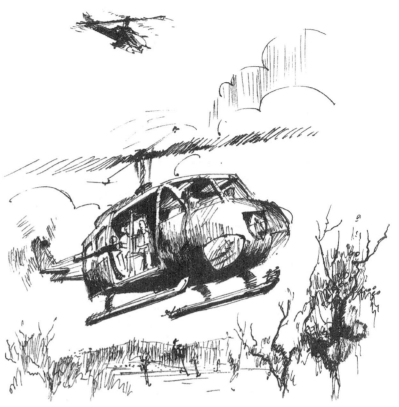

Helicopters on patrol

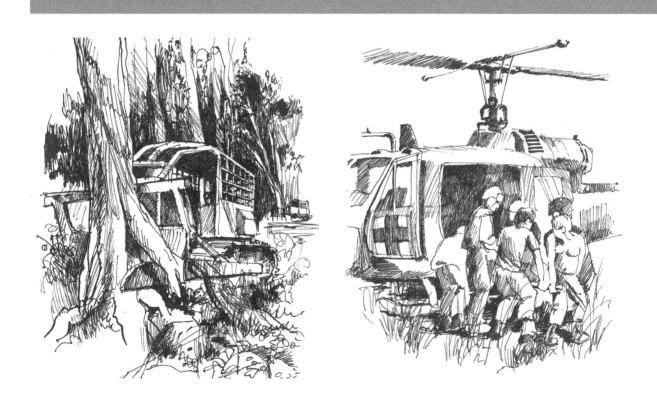

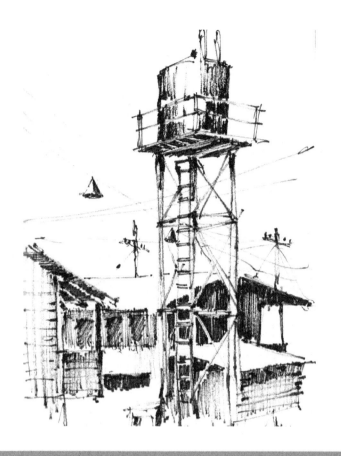

" I lived for six months on the second floor of this wooden barracks, which was typical of centralized military base housing in Vietnam.

A quick sketch illustrating a typical Vietnam scene—lush vegetation, wide rivers and people transporting goods to market in their boats.

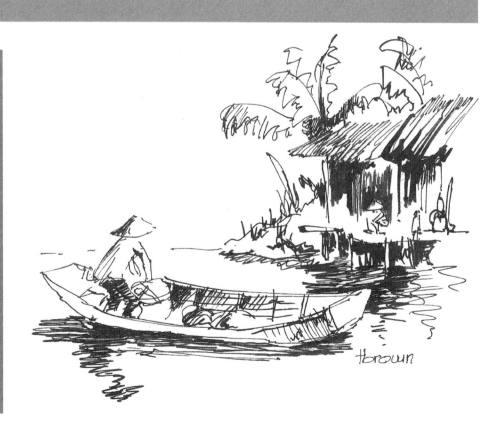

"Dublin Castle"
Bunker

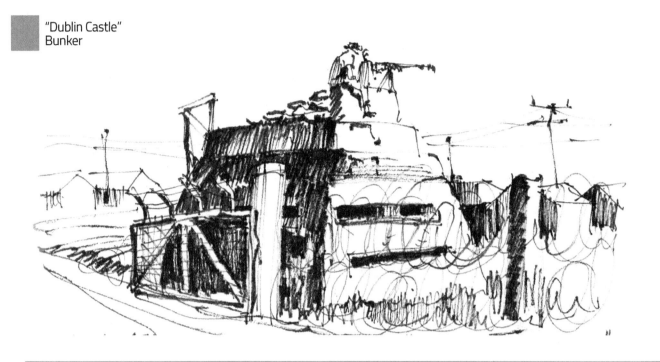

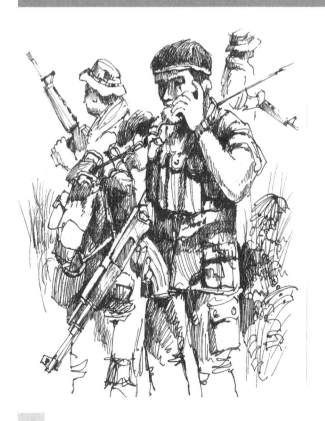

∧ Soldier on Radio

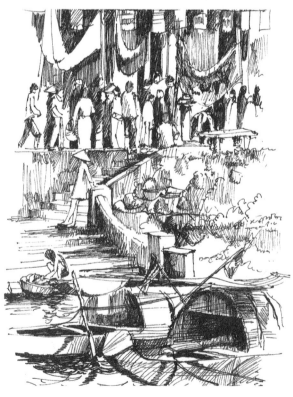

∧ Riverside Party

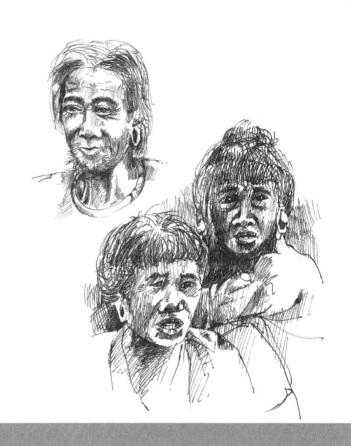

"

Montagnard
(mountain) people from
the Central Highlands
fought alongside US
Special forces in the
Vietnam War.

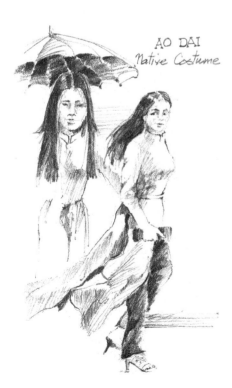

AO DAI
Native Costume

Ao Dai
Womens Dress

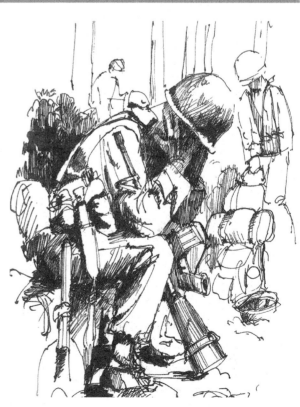

End of
Mission

SRI LANKA

A rich history and colorful scenes kept me drawing despite often being overwhelmed by damage from the tsunami. Many of my drawings were completed during the flight home.

Early in 2005, while serving as Chair of the American Institute of Architects Disaster Assistance Committee, I mobilized a team of architects, engineers, landscape architects, planners and civil engineers to visit Sri Lanka and study damage caused by the 2004 Indian Ocean earthquake and tsunami that smashed into the coast of this island country. We arrived in Colombo, Sri Lanka late at night and were greeted by officials of the Sri Lanka Institute of Architects.

Our goal was to observe the damage and effects of the tsunami that devastated the coastal areas of eleven Asian countries, including most of the coastline of Sri Lanka. After visiting with various state ministries in Colombo, the capitol city, we traveled a narrow two-lane coastal road in a small bus, driven by a man who removed his sandals and drove bare foot. He constantly honked his horn at anyone driving a motorcycle or tractor who were in his way.

It was heart wrenching to see the destruction of the coastal areas. Thousands of people, especially, the families of poor fishermen who lived along the coast lost everything including their lives. At one point, we stopped to visit badly damaged train cars that were placed back on the tracks as a memorial to the estimated 1,700 passengers who were killed. The overcrowded passenger train was broad sided by the giant tsunami waves making it the single worst rail disaster in world history. The Sri Lanka Architects

wanted us to also see some of the beauty of their country so we stopped to visit various important sites, to include the historic Portuguese town of Galle and its prestigious lighthouse. Best of all, was the visit to Sigiriya, or Lion Rock, an enormous rock outcropping which is said to have housed a king's palace on the top. About half way up the side of the cliff is a distinctive gateway in the form of a lion.

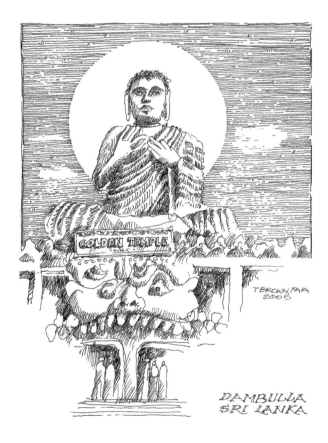

DAMBULLA
SRI LANKA

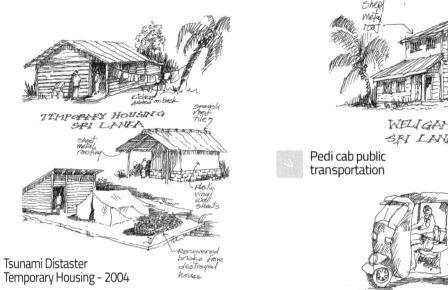

Tsunami Distaster
Temporary Housing - 2004

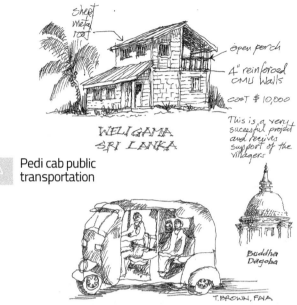

Pedi cab public
transportation

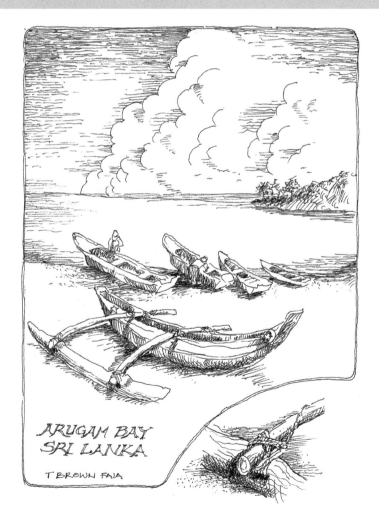

> Fishermen left their boats on the beach and carried their heavy outboard boat motors on their shoulders to their houses.

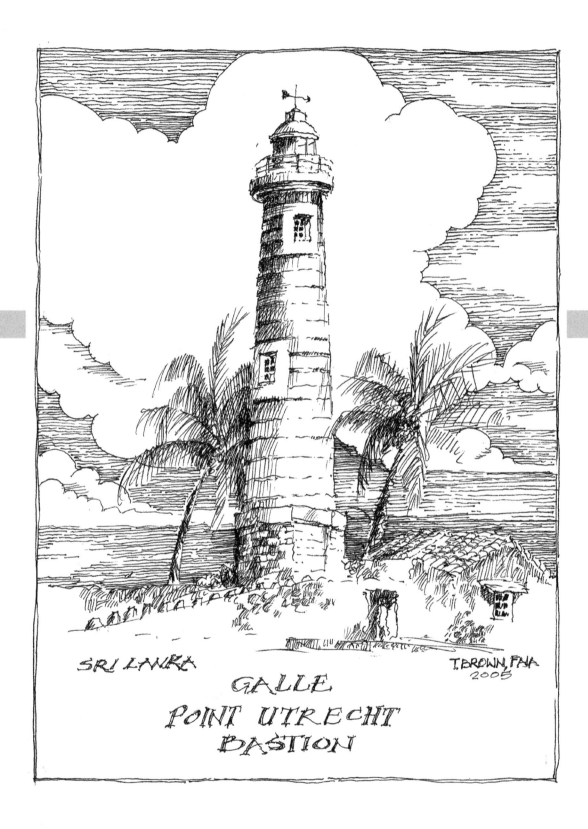

SRI LANKA

GALLE
POINT UTRECHT
BASTION

T. BROWN, FAIA
2005

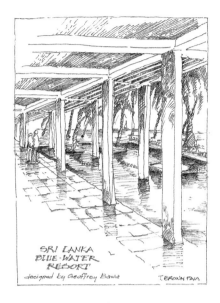

SRI LANKA
BLUE-WATER
RESORT
designed by Geoffrey Bawa
T.BROWN FAIA

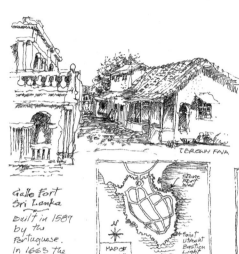

Galle Fort
Sri Lanka
built in 1589
by the
Portuguese.
In 1663 the
Dutch built the
36 hectare fort

MAP OF
GALLE

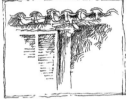

Galle Fort
built 1589

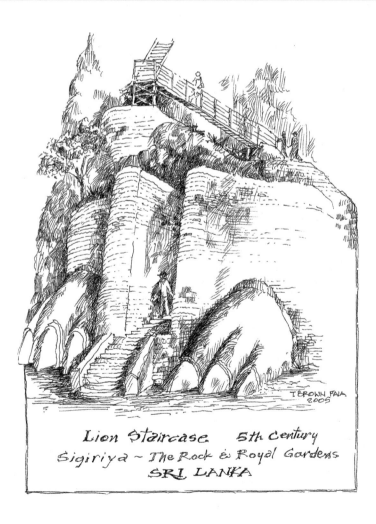

Lion Staircase   5th Century
Sigiriya ~ The Rock & Royal Gardens
SRI LANKA

> "
> A stone fortress
> called Sigiriya
> sits in the heart
> of Sri Lanka. This
> spectacular
> red brick Lion
> Staircase
> guarded entry
> to the spindly
> metal stairs above
> and uppermost
> hanging walkways.

TURKEY

Minarets and domed mosques pierce the sky in every town and city I traveled, as revealed in my sketches.

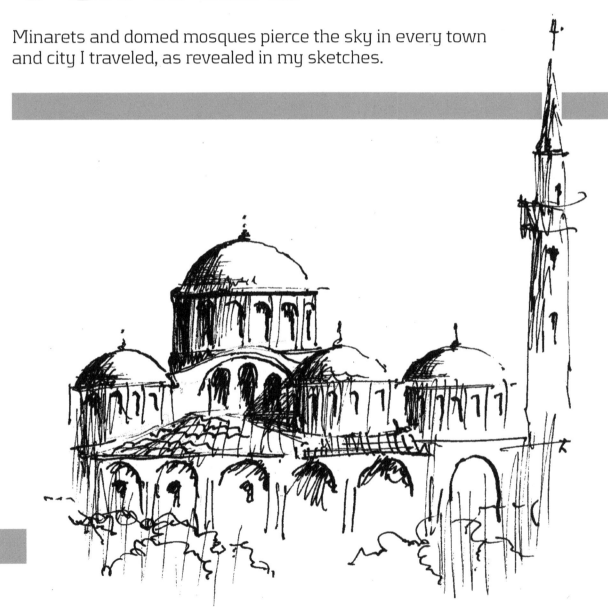

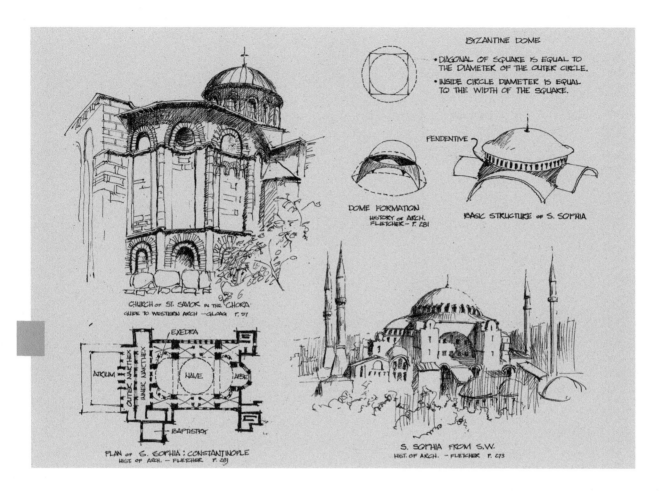

BYZANTINE DOME
• DIAGONAL OF SQUARE IS EQUAL TO THE DIAMETER OF THE OUTER CIRCLE.
• INSIDE CIRCLE DIAMETER IS EQUAL TO THE WIDTH OF THE SQUARE.

PENDENTIVE

DOME FORMATION
HISTORY OF ARCH. FLETCHER - P. 281

BASIC STRUCTURE OF S. SOPHIA

CHURCH OF ST. SAVIOR IN THE CHORA
GUIDE TO WESTERN ARCH - GLAAG P. 57

PLAN OF S. SOPHIA : CONSTANTINOPLE
HIST. OF ARCH. - FLETCHER P. 281

S. SOPHIA FROM S.W.
HIST. OF ARCH. - FLETCHER P. 273

Driving across Turkey was a unique experience with skylines punctured by minarets, sights, and smells that I had never-before experienced. At one point I was exhausted and let the car's owner drive for a while, but when he needed to refuel, he pulled into a roadside gas station, and nearly crashed into a gas pump. I never let him drive after that.

The markets were crowded and each time I stopped to look at something in a merchant's stall, he waved his hand and a young boy carrying hot tea in little glasses showed up to serve me. One time, I stopped to eat lunch at a small one room restaurant where the cook had a rectangular raised area in the corner with stews simmering in pots on a bed of charcoal. Sheep and goat heads hung on the rack above so I knew he served mutton. I sat down at a small table and noticed a fingerprinted decanter of

water and four grease smudged drinking glasses. I decided to order a Coke and drank out of the bottle. The floor had a layer of water all over it and the cook worked barefooted with his shoes leaning up against the wall with the toes pointed up. It did not take long for me to figure out why there was water on the floor. Two Turkish men sat down at the table beside me, poured water from the decanter in their glasses, swirled it around and dumped the water on the floor. I guess they felt that cleaned the glasses.

The most notable structure in Istanbul was the immense Hagia Sophia Museum. It was originally built as an Orthodox Christian Church with its massive-relatively-flat Byazntine dome. The minarets, or prayer towers, were built after it became a Muslim mosque.

EGYPT & THE MIDDLE EAST

The drawings in this section were illustrated while I was a twenty-one-year old college student studying architectural history. I had a general knowledge of ancient Egypt, pharaohs, pyramids and the Nile River, learned from movies and school, however, studying ancient Egyptian architectural history in college was a real eye opener. Early Egyptian architecture, giant sculpture and tombs enthralled me. It was interesting to learn that wood was so scarce, stone was used for building most parts of the tombs, temples columns and even roofs. Palaces and most other structures to include walls were often built with bricks. Some of the pyramid's cores were built of stone and brick and were often faced with smooth limestone, which over the centuries, was removed to construct buildings in nearby Cairo. There are over eighty pyramids in Egypt and all of them are over three thousand years old. They were built as the burial places for the mummified remains of the Pharaohs. The pyramids were often constructed with multiple tunnels to thwart robbers who, even in ancient times, searched for Pharaohs' remains and sold the mummies and tomb's contents for great sums.

The earliest pyramids were built in the form of giant steps like the stepped Ziggurat of Ur-Nammu in Iraq, illustrated in this section. The largest pyramid is the Great Pyramid at Giza which is a shape we are most familiar with, a true four-sided pyramid. It is the oldest and largest in the world. Pyramids and giant structures of Egypt are a testament to the power of the pharaohs and their quest to have their names last forever. The pharaohs also built giant statues and tombs of stone to include the massive Great Sphinx which is a mythical form of a lion laying down with a human head. Napoleons soldiers are reputed to have used the Sphinx head for target practice. The nose is missing and the eyes are severely damaged.

After studying the classical column capitols of ancient Greece and Rome, I was amazed to learn the Egyptian column capitols were often carved in the form of a lotus blossom. This water-loving plant commonly grows along the Nile river where Egyptian civilization has flourished for thousands of years.

In this section, you will also find drawings of Bronze Age Mycenaean structures built on mainland Greece between 1,600–1,100 BCE and the architecture of Persia. (modern-day Iran) circa 2,500 BCE, and extending into the Mesopotamia Valley, which is thought to be the "cradle of civilization." Craftsmen carved fluted stone columns and crowned them with double-bull capitals. It saddens me to learn that, modern terrorists have destroyed some of these buildings, the most ancient structures on earth. They stood for thousands of years, a testament to the builders who created them.

EGYPT & THE MIDDLE EAST

The process of researching and drawing these ancient ruins opened my eyes to the unique skill of Egyptian architects and artists.

The ancient ruins of Egypt and the Middle East have always amazed me, partly due to their age and the crude tools and slave labor required for their construction. The pyramids are now a World Heritage Site. The scale of these monumental stone buildings is magnificent, and the stone carver's attention to detail is inspiring. I created these sketches while studying architectural history. I emulated drawings done by Sir Banister Fletcher in his book titled *Architecture History on the Comparative Method.* I was surprised to learn that the Egyptians created their culture's unique columns and capitals based on the shapes of palm, papyrus and lotus blossoms.

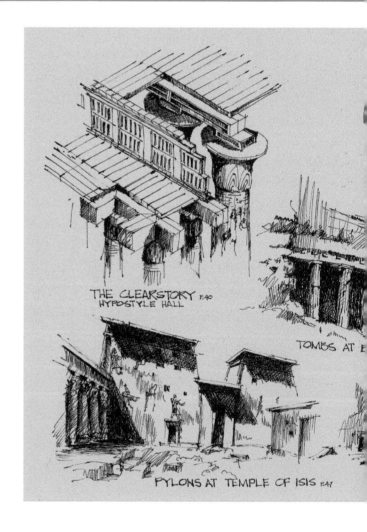

THE CLEARSTORY P.40
HYPOSTYLE HALL

TOMBS AT B

PYLONS AT TEMPLE OF ISIS P.41

> The Great Sphinx
Giza, Egypt

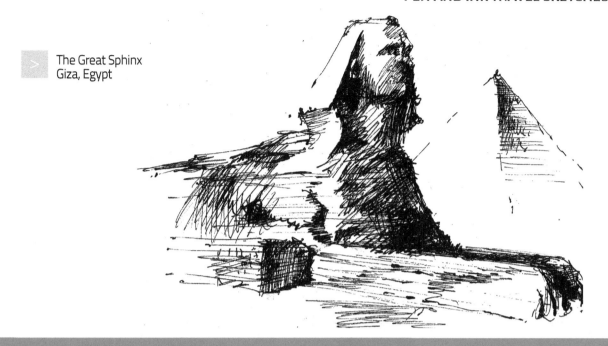

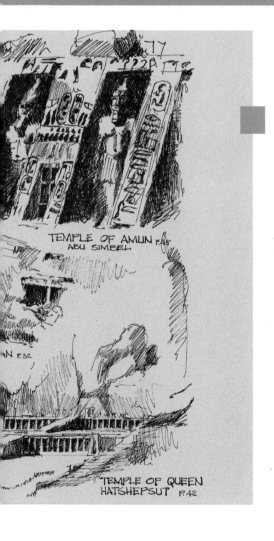

TEMPLE OF AMUN P.45
ABU SIMBEL

N P.32

TEMPLE OF QUEEN
HATSHEPSUT P.42

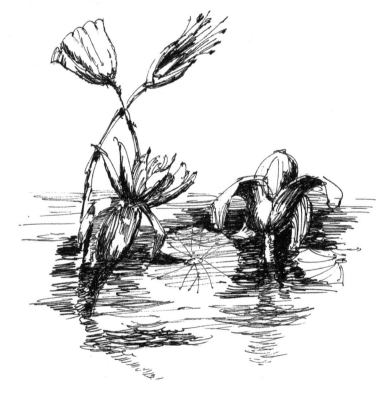

NATURAL LOTUS IN BUD,
BLOSSOM AND SEED POD P. 177
REF. — EGYPT AND ITS MONUMENTS by AMELIA EDWARDS

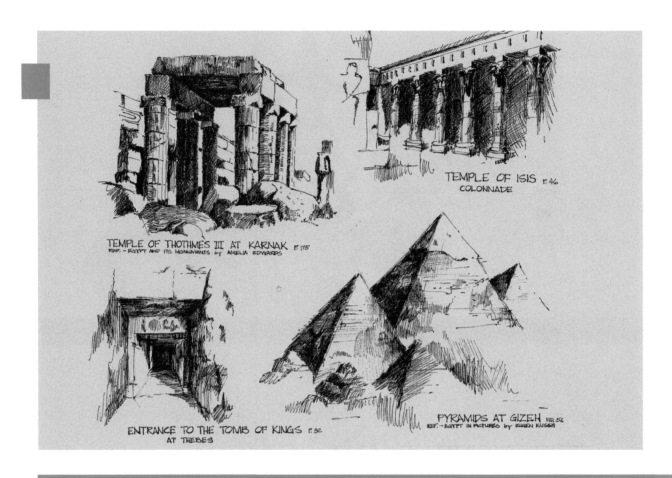

TEMPLE OF ISIS P. 46
COLONNADE

TEMPLE OF THOTHMES III AT KARNAK P. 175
REF. – EGYPT AND ITS MONUMENTS by AMELIA EDWARDS

ENTRANCE TO THE TOMB OF KINGS P. 32
AT THEBES

PYRAMIDS AT GIZEH NO. 52
REF. – EGYPT IN PICTURES by EUGEN KUSCH

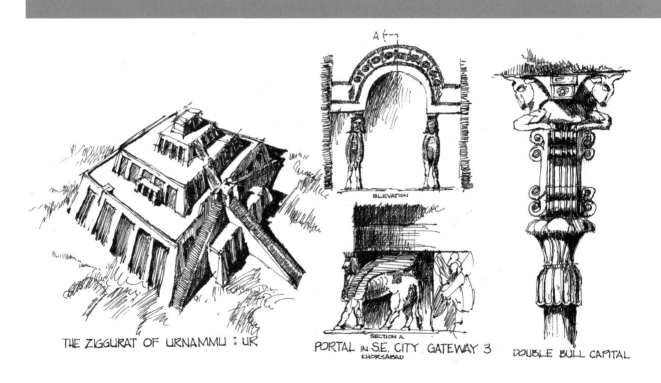

THE ZIGGURAT OF URNAMMU : UR

ELEVATION

SECTION A

PORTAL IN S.E. CITY GATEWAY 3
KHORSABAD

DOUBLE BULL CAPITAL

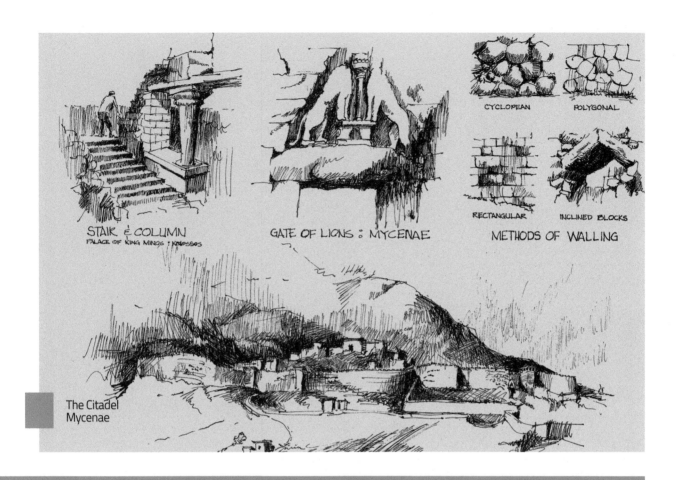

STAIR & COLUMN
PALACE OF KING MINOS : KNOSSOS

GATE OF LIONS : MYCENAE

METHODS OF WALLING

CYCLOPEAN   POLYGONAL

RECTANGULAR   INCLINED BLOCKS

The Citadel
Mycenae

> " Fragments of large scale urban settlements on the lower Euphrates River around 2,500 BCE, mark some of the earliest civilizations on earth.

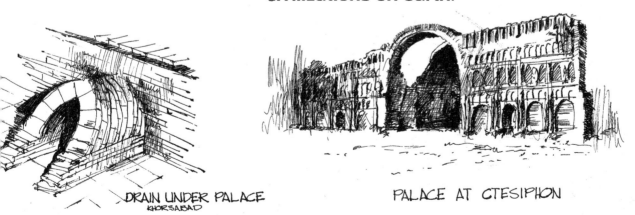

DRAIN UNDER PALACE
KHORSABAD

PALACE AT CTESIPHON

SOUTH AMERICA

Several of these drawings were made during my 1971–1972 travels through Argentina, Bolivia, Brazil, Chile, Colombia, Ecuador and Peru. The others were drawn during recent trips to these countries. In the 1970s, I did not plan to travel this deep into Latin America, but I just kept drifting South. I began my travels in Montana, then traveled across the USA and Mexico to Guatemala where I studied Spanish. A couple from Canada, who I met in Guatemala, offered to take me in their Volkswagen bus to Panama. I then caught a plane to Medellin, Columbia where my passport was stolen almost as soon as I landed, which forced me to stay in Bogota for twenty-two days waiting until I could get a new passport.

I originally toyed with the idea of boating down the wild Amazon River to the Atlantic coast, but I had just spent a year in Vietnam jungles and did not want to repeat a jungle experience. In Columbia, I met a fellow traveler who recommended I explore South America by traveling through the Andean Republics in lieu of beginning my South American exploration from Brazil. The Andean weather is much cooler and the mountainous countryside has exhilarating views. So, I began a long trip through the Andes Mountains traveling in rattle-trap buses over single lane gravel and stone roads with steep drop-offs winding through the mountains. Along the way, there were way-points where the bus would stop and the driver's helper collected coins from the passengers and ran out to place them in a box posted at precarious drop offs. In some way, they believed this gesture was a gesture to God to protect us along the way. What probably happens is that the helper pads his pocket under the guise of providing us with safe passage.

The journey between Bogota, Columbia to Quito, Ecuador was grueling, but worth the effort. Quito is a beautiful, friendly city with an historic city center crowded with gilded Spanish Colonial churches and tile roof buildings. The drawings of Quito were made during one of my later trips to Ecuador.

My next stop was Lima, Peru to visit the historic Spanish Colonial Capitol of South America, founded by the Conquistador Francisco Pizarro, who conquered the Inca in 1533. Pizarro executed the last emperor of the Inca, marking the end of three hundred years of Inca rule. The Inca people still make up a heavy portion of the Peruvian population. In 1892, a corpse thought to be that of Pizarro, was exhumed and put on display in a glass coffin, and beset with curiosity, I had to see it. Years later, it was determined that the remains on display was not that of Pizarro.

Several friends found a hand drawn map in the Cuzco travel office, which indicated a 54 kilometer Inca road system through the Andes ending at the ruins of Machu Pichu, the most familiar icon of Inca civilization located on a high ridge above the Urubamba River. The Spaniards searched for this fabled village, but never found it. We decided to hike the trail and packed for the six-day trip. The mountains were exceedingly steep forcing us to stop every few steps because of the lack of oxygen. It took seven grueling hours to reach the first ridge. After five days of hiking we arrived at the Inca masterpiece of community design on the top of a mountain ridge.

After returning to Lima, I traveled by train up the torturous mountain side to the Inca market in Huancayo. The mountain was so steep the train had to lumber up the mountain on tracks built with switchbacks. The train would travel first in one direction then up backwards the next section until we reached the top. At that altitude, the air was so thin it made people lightheaded. To counter that, a conductor passed through the train cars administering oxygen to passengers in need. Cuzco, the ancient city of Inca where one senses the ancient Inca who battled the Spaniards, is a beautiful example of Inca craftsmanship. The perfection of Inca stone work where craftsmen fitted giant boulders together without mortar is stunning.

I turned twenty-seven while traveling in Bolivia. La Paz, the capitol and the country's largest city, looked like a giant bowl of houses and humanity. It was apparent to me that the wealthy people lived in the lower part of the city and the poorer ones lived in rustic houses high up on the hill sides.

While on a twenty-six-hour dusty bus ride to the southern border of Bolivia we stopped to pick up passengers and a woman and her daughter sat down beside me. Somewhere, miles down the road, she screamed something about me having her seat and stabbed me in the leg with a crochet hook. I hollered and pushed her hard and somehow the crochet hook was driven through her thumb, exiting below her thumbnail. I did not have her seat, but decided it was best to let her and her daughter have it and spent the rest of the trip eating dust in the back of the bus.

From Bolivia, I rode trains to Buenos Aires, Argentina and calculated, up to that point, I spent about four dollars a day or a hundred and twenty dollars a month for most of my travels. Argentina would turn out to be even less expensive. I ate a T-Bone steak dinner for 5 1/2 cents U.S. A large pizza cost twenty cents. I reached Buenos Aires, the capitol of Argentina in 1972 after a year-long arduous but exciting journey from Montana. I decided to settle awhile, rest, improve my Spanish and found a job in the architectural studio of Argentina's foremost architect, Clorindo Testa, designing a new seaside community called Pinamar, south of Buenos Aires

along the Atlantic coast. My stay in Hotel Victory cost twenty dollars a month. Three months later, my friend Danelle, who I traveled with in Mexico and Guatemala, arrived in Buenos Aires and we hit the road to explore Chile and the Argentine Patagonia.

Chile is a long narrow country with the Pacific Ocean alongside the entire western coast and the towering Andes Mountains on the east, isolating it from the rest of South America. Because of this, I found the Chilean people to be extremely welcoming and friendly. We hitchhiked south to the road's end and steamed along the Southern coast aboard a passenger ship following the Chilean coast to Punta Arenas in the Strait of Magellan. After landing, we hitchhiked to Ushuaia, Tierra del Fuego, the southernmost town in the world. Then we continued to the end of the road, as far south as one can travel by land in South America, and camped under a shelter in a National Park. At that point we were close to Antarctica. We had been traveling for a year and three months.

After bearing winter conditions, we hitchhiked back to Buenos Aires across the wild and barren Patagonia on the eastern side of the Andes. The round-trip excursion from Buenos Aires to Tierra del Fuego took three months and cost me thirty dollars. Danelle and I stayed with friends in Buenos Aires for a while, then I set off by myself hitchhiking across Uruguay, Paraguay, and Brazil to Rio de Janeiro. By that time, I was running low on money and decided to buy a plane ticket with the remainder of my funds to Mexico with a stopover in Brasilia, the new capital of Brazil, then back to Guatemala where I studied Spanish on my way south. I figured that with the remaining fifty dollars I could hitchhike from Mexico City to my brother's house in Lubbock, Texas. As it turned out, I wound up staying in Guatemala for eight years.

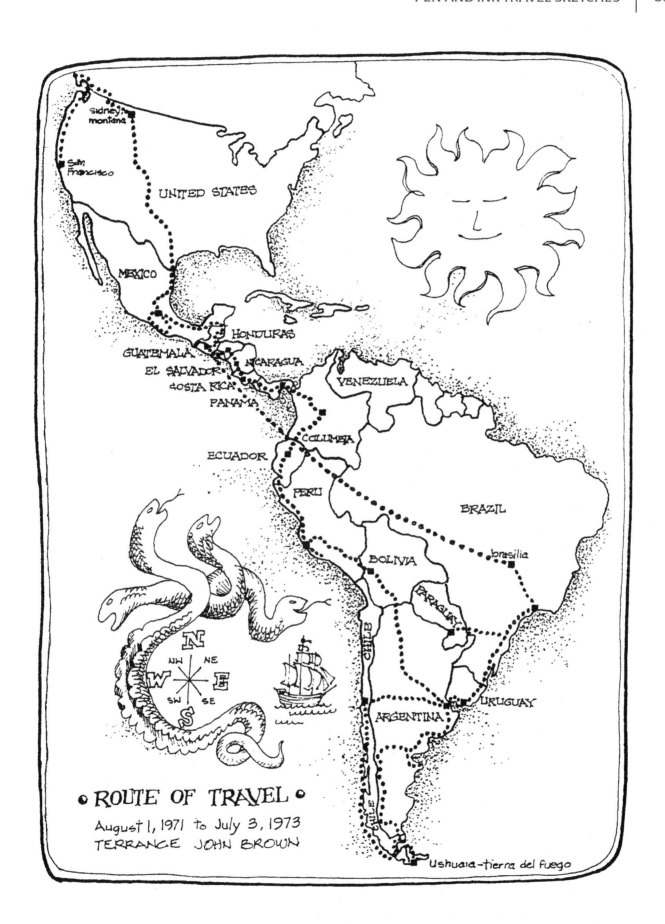

● ROUTE OF TRAVEL ●
August 1, 1971 to July 3, 1973
TERRANCE JOHN BROWN

ARGENTINA

Argentina provided many opportunities to sketch. Along the way I became intrigued by the distinctive cowboys, or gauchos, of the Patagonia.

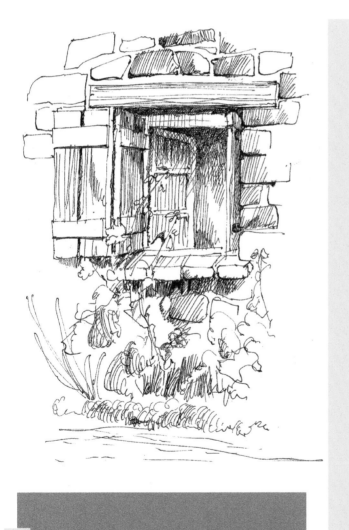

Window Detail
Bariloche, Argentina

After serving in Vietnam, I traveled mostly by land from my home in Montana to Buenos Aires, Argentina. An architectural student, who I met on a train in northern Argentina, suggested I talk to Argentina's famous architect, Clorindo Testa. After a short visit, Mr. Testa gave me a job designing a resort community at Pinamar, along the Atlantic coast. I lived in the turn of the century Hotel Victory in a Buenos Aires suburb and rode a commuter train and bus to work. After three months I packed it up and traveled across the Andes to Santiago, Chile. I found the book titled *The Gaucho Martin Fierro*, by Jose Hernandez, about Patagonia intriguing, so I continued my exploration across the southern regions of South America. I crossed the Straights of Magellan and traveled to Ushuaia, the southernmost city in the world.

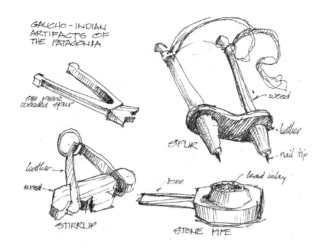

Gaucho
Artifacts

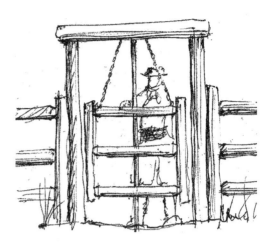

Self Closing Gate
Punta Angostara

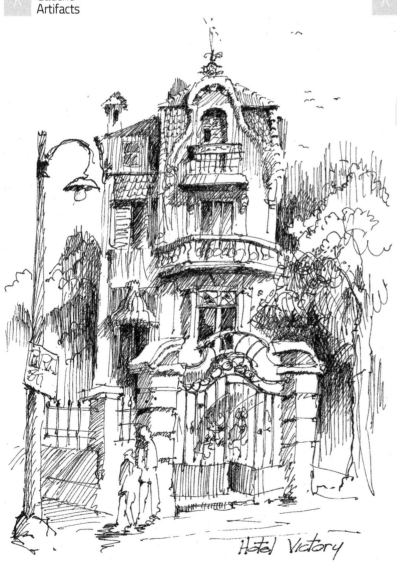

"

European
immigrants often
influenced the
design of buildings
in Buenos Aires to
appear similar to
the buildings of their
home.

The Hotel Victory
Buenos Aries

BRAZIL

The first of my four trips to Brazil came at the end of a year and a half exploration of Central and South America.

I traveled over land from Uruguay to Rio de Janiero in 1973, yet created only one drawing during the trip—of the statue of Christ on Sugarloaf Mountain. I was exhausted, nearly broke and on the last leg of my year and a half exploration of the region. However, over the last few years, I ventured to numerous cities along the coast while serving as the American Institute of Architects Liaison to the Federation of Pan American Architects Associations. My last trip to Brazil was a disaster. The immigration officer in Sao Paulo refused me entry to Brazil on my valid visa because my passport had expired 5 days earlier. Immigration kept me in the airport for 10 hours, giving me time to do many airport scene sketches. They eventually put me a flight back to Chicago.

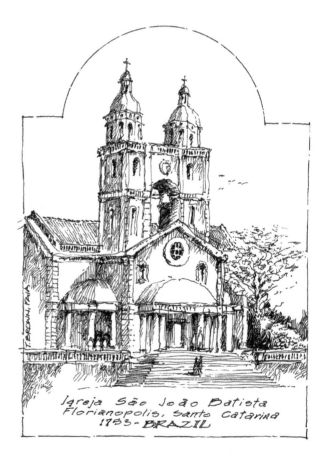

Igreja São João Batista
Florianopolis, Santo Catarina
1983 - BRAZIL

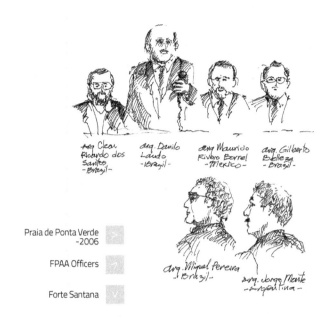

Arq. Clear Ricardo dos Santos -Brazil-

arq. Danilo Lando -Brazil-

arq. Mauricio Rivera Borrel -Mexico-

arq. Gilberto Belleza -Brazil-

arq. Miguel Pereira -Brazil-

arq. Jorge Monte -Argentina-

Praia de Ponta Verde -2006

FPAA Officers

Forte Santana

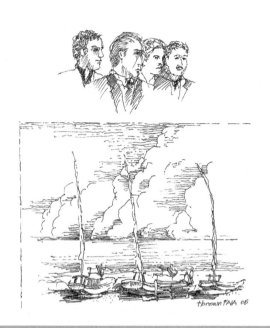

tbrown FAIA 05

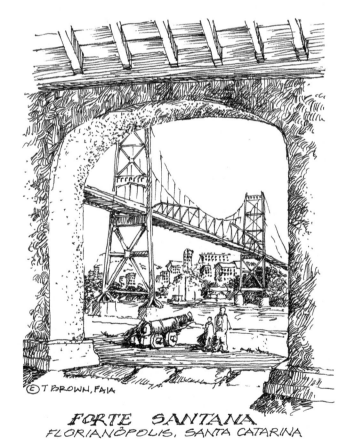

© T BROWN, FAIA

FORTE SANTANA
FLORIANÓPOLIS, SANTA CATARINA
BRASIL

"

While drawing the bridge framed in the doorway, I was quickly surrounded by excited school children eager to see what I was doing. I drew a small portrait of one of them and of course they all wanted one then.

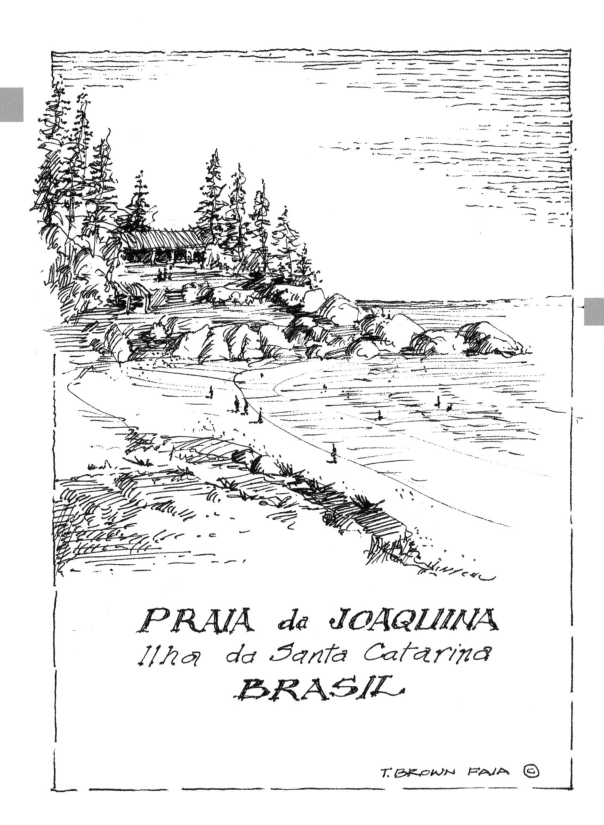

PRAIA da JOAQUINA
Ilha da Santa Catarina
BRASIL

T. BROWN FAIA ©

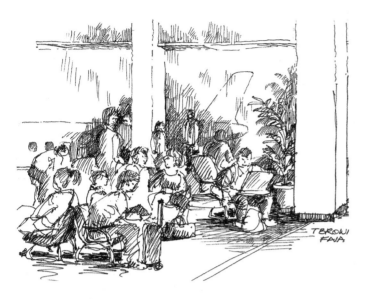

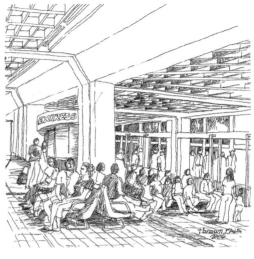

Sao Paulo Airport Brazil
-2006

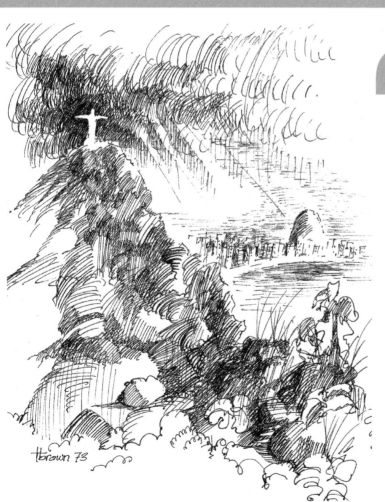

The drawing of the famous statue of Christ the Redeemer watching over Rio de Janeiro was made from a magazine photograph and is the last drawing I made before leaving South America.

 Rio de Janiero
-1973

CHILE

Traveling from one end of this county to the other presents countless opportunities to practice drawing boats.

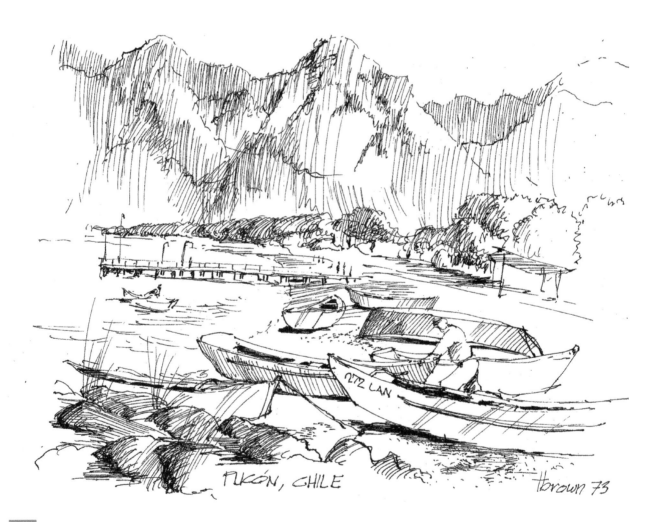

PUCÓN, CHILE

tbrown 73

Pucon, Chili
-1973

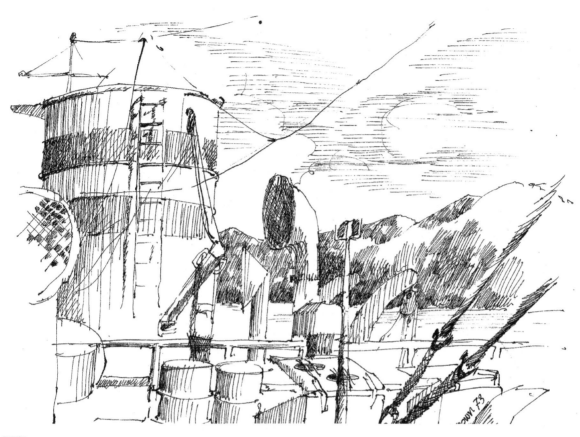

∧ Navarino Boat in Southern Chile
-1973

Geographically, Chile is a elongated, narrow country isolated by the Andes Mountains to the east and the Pacific Ocean on the west. Chileans are very friendly and eager to talk to outsiders. I traveled to Puerto Mont, as far south as the road would go, then boarded a passenger boat and steamed along the coast to the Straights of Magellan and Tierra del Fuego. On the way, the boat anchored in a fiord and fishermen from a village rowed out to meet us holding up giant crabs for sale. Many of the remote houses in this part of the world have exterior walls covered with intricate patterned cedar shingles.

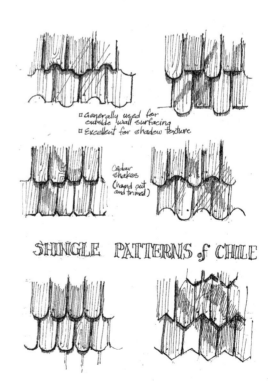

□ Generally used for outside wall surfacing
□ Excellent for shadow texture

Cedar shakes (hand cut and trimed)

SHINGLE PATTERNS of CHILE

COLUMBIA

After my passport was stolen in Medellin, my first stop in a tour of South America, I sketched and stayed a month in a cheap Bogota hotel while waiting for the US Embassy to provide a new one.

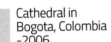

Cathedral in
Bogota, Colombia
-2006

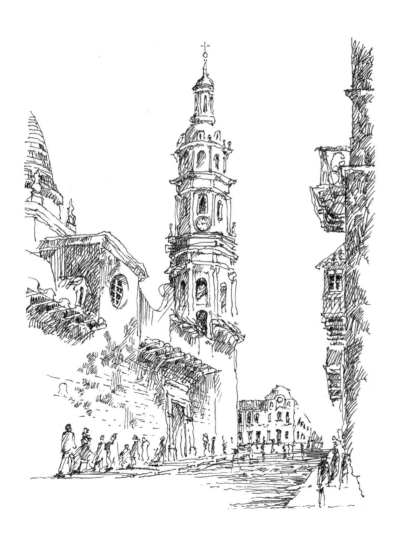

From the vantage point of my hotel room, I could only see a portion of the adjacent highrise. Also, the mountain was covered in fog for two days, so I couldn't finish the drawing until the clouds cleared. Despite my awareness of Colombia's recent history of kidnapping, I decided to leave the hotel and tour Bogota. A Colombian architecture student drove me to the city's main plaza. This large, open public space is a stunning sight, as is the immense scale of its cathedral and the cathedral's single bell tower. I sketched the drawing while standing in front of a side street restaurant, where we had a flavorful lunch.

Church Roof Detail
Bogota-2006

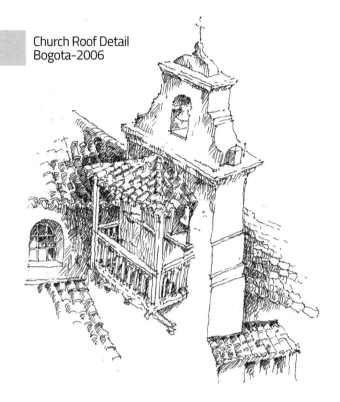

The gold museum in Bogota displays stunning examples of Inca archaeological and artistic artwork. One room was lined with shimmering gold treasures across its ceiling and all four walls.

Bogota, Colombia
-2006

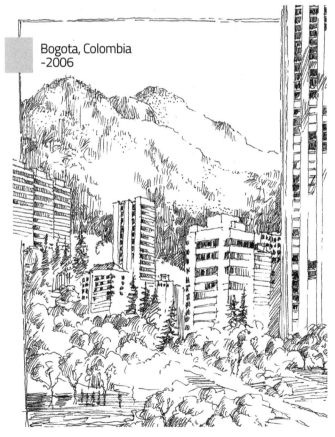

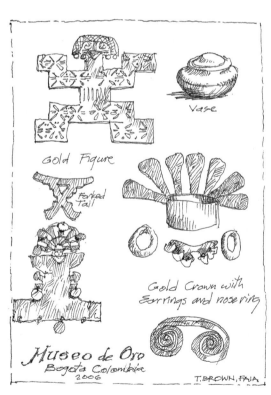

Museum de Oro
Bogota, Colombia -2004

ECUADOR

The heart of the capital city of Quito is loaded with Spanish Colonial buildings and churches, providing me with endless drawing opportunities.

Quito is a beautiful and historic capital. The Spanish Colonial influence on its architecture and culture is pronounced. In Ecuador, Columbia, Peru and Bolivia, I traversed the Andes—the longest continental mountain range in the world—in rickety school buses. The travel was dusty, bone rattling and often perilous, with precipitous heights, hair-pin turns and poorly maintained roads. The bus often stopped at a dangerous curve and the driver's helper would jump out and supposedly deposit coins in a metal box. The boy collected the money from the passengers as a gift to the Gods to keep us safe on our journey though the mountains.

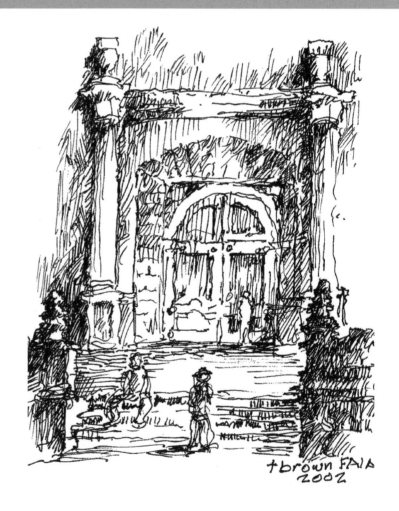

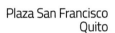

Plaza San Francisco
Quito

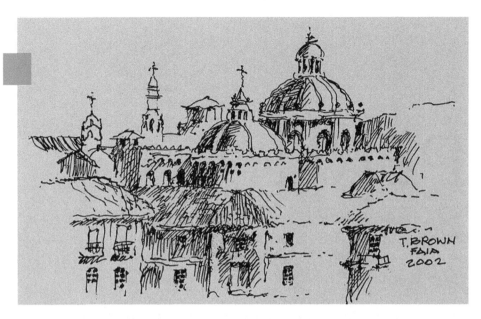

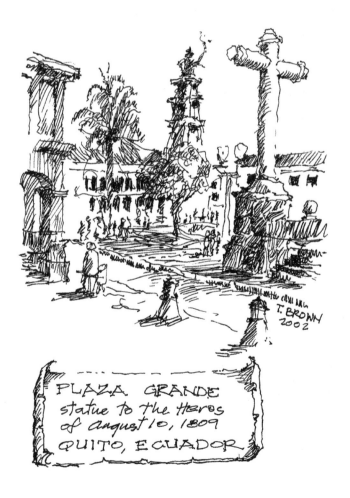

"

Quitos' numerous domed Spanish Colonial churches, with their interiors encrusted in gold, appear to be the most ornate in Latin America.

PLAZA GRANDE
statue to the Heroes
of August 10, 1809
QUITO, ECUADOR

PERU

The luggage I carried—actually just a single leather bag—while traveling through the Americas held all my personal items. A gourd served as my canteen. The jungle boots I wore were issued to me while serving in Vietnam.

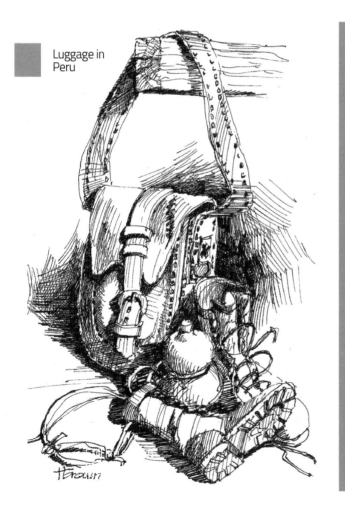

Luggage in
Peru

After my perilous journey across the Andes from Ecuador, I arrived in Lima, the capital of Peru, and stayed a few days in a small hotel in the old part of the city. I sketched the Rio Rimac Bridge and a few of Lima's historic buildings from the hotel balcony. Then I traveled by train on switchback tracks up the Andes to Cuzco, where I befriended three other travelers. We trekked for five days along an Inca trail system that led us over some of the highest mountains in South America. After our last day of hiking, night was closing in and we were in the vicinity of the fabled Inca ruins of Machu Picchu, so we camped on the mountain top. The next morning, Machu Picchu appeared like a jewel amidst a setting of mountain peaks high above the Urubamba River.

Machu Pichu
Peru

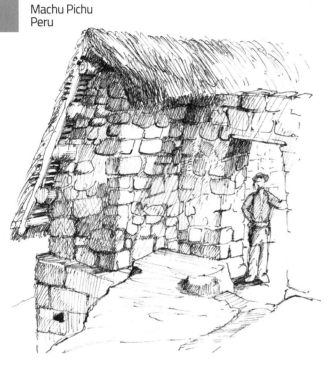

"

Machu Pichu was so well hidden high atop the Andes that Spanish conqueror's never located the stone community. Thus it remains intact, with angled thatched roofs that mimick the steep slope of the mountains.

Rio Rimac
Lima, Peru

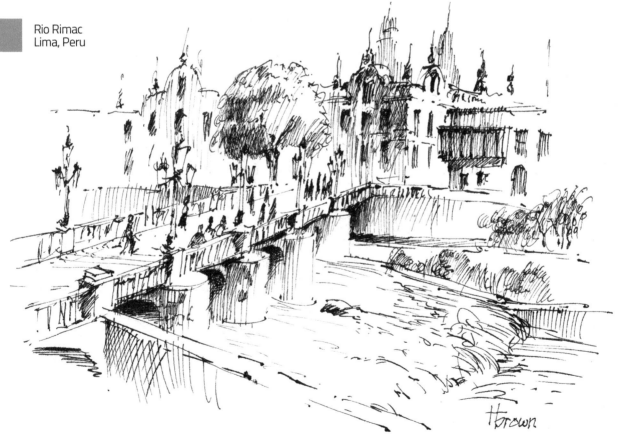

CENTRAL AMERICA and MEXICO

After returning home from the Vietnam War in 1971, I had difficulty concentrating and had no interest in settling down to an eight to five job. I was staying with my parents in Montana and had the urge to explore. My college friend, Danelle Crowley, wrote me and suggested that we travel to Latin America. She had been serving as a Peace Corp Volunteer in Panama and planned to travel to South America after her Peace Corp service but was sent back to the states for medical treatment.

Not to be convinced otherwise, I agreed, and set off with my sketch book to explore Latin America with a $1,000 of combat pay tucked into my boot top and a passport. I was excited to be alive and looked forward to the experience. I drove from Montana to Lubbock, Texas then traveled from Danelle's home in Dimmitt, Texas into Mexico. We traveled with another friend of hers in his van, camping along the way. We explored various pre-Columbian archaeological sites such as Teotihuacan, the largest Mesoamerican city in the Americas covering eight square miles. It's massive main road through the center of the ancient city measured a staggering 131 feet wide and three miles long. The Aztecs called this road Avenue of the Dead because of the buildings lining the avenue looked as if they were tombs.

After exploring another large pre-Colombian archaeological site called Monte Alban, in the state of Oaxaca, we were eager to see the ocean so we followed a long winding road down the mountain, arriving late at night, to a small beach town called Puerto Angel and decided to sleep on the beach. The next morning, we found that thieves had broken into the van and stole nearly everything except what we had with us, passports, money and sleeping bags, on the beach. They left my Vietnam combat boots and a pair of jeans. Danelle fared the same which really lightened our load. I bought a cotton flower sack to carry what few things I had left.

Not long after that, the van's owner decided to return to the States saying he had mechanical troubles. That left us hitchhiking across the southern neck of Mexico to the small country of Belize along the Caribbean coast. A Belizean border guard told me to put my luggage on the table in front of him and I put my sack of belonging there and my sleeping bag. He exclaimed "that's all you have? Then he handed my passport back saying he did not want me in his country. I was astonished and said "I served as a US Army officer in the Vietnam War and because I was robbed of all my possessions in Mexico, your telling me you forbid us entry into your country?" He exclaimed, you served in Vietnam? and took our passports and stamped three-day passes, enough to cross Belize to Guatemala.

We traveled by bus across the Peten jungle to Tikal, the massive Mayan city complex with the tops of temples poking through the top of the jungle canopy. After exploring the ruins we spent a rainy night sleeping in a remote gas station. Danelle slept on cardboard boxes spread over the oil drenched floor and I spread my sleeping bag on the counter. The next day we rode in an old bus to the market in Guatemala City with fat squealing pigs tied to the top of the bus's roof. People inside held chickens, ducks and small animals for the market.

I n Antigua, Guatemala, we looked up Danelle's friend Jo Froman, who completed Peace Corp training with her. Jo, along with Bob Gersony, and Tony Jackson, founded a non-profit linguistics center called Proyecto Lingüístico Francisco Marroquín (PLFM). This center aimed at revitalizing the use of the country's twenty Mayan languages spoken by more than half the population. I studied Spanish intensively for five days a week, one on one, for two months while living with a Guatemalan family who spoke no English which forced me to buckle down to learn the language.

From Antigua, I traveled with a Canadian couple in their van across Central America to Panama City. I camped out each night along the way across El Salvador, Honduras, Nicaragua, Costa Rica to Panama. Then I flew from Panama City to Medallin, Colombia.

After traveling for a year and a half in South America, I arrived back in Guatemala. My friends at the PLFM, asked me to serve as an integral part of the team which managed the first language school in Antigua and lead the team to create two new language schools and cultural learning centers, in the distant highland towns of Huehuetenango and Quetzaltenango. The schools taught Spanish and cultural adaptation to international development technicians, researchers, missionaries and volunteers assigned to work throughout Latin America. I assisted thousands of men and women of all ages, national origins, linguistic capabilities and backgrounds to make a successful and comfortable cultural adjustment to Latin America. These Spanish Schools continue to operate today.

"

As it turned out, I wound up traveling in Latin America for a year and a half, then lived in Guatemala for eight years.

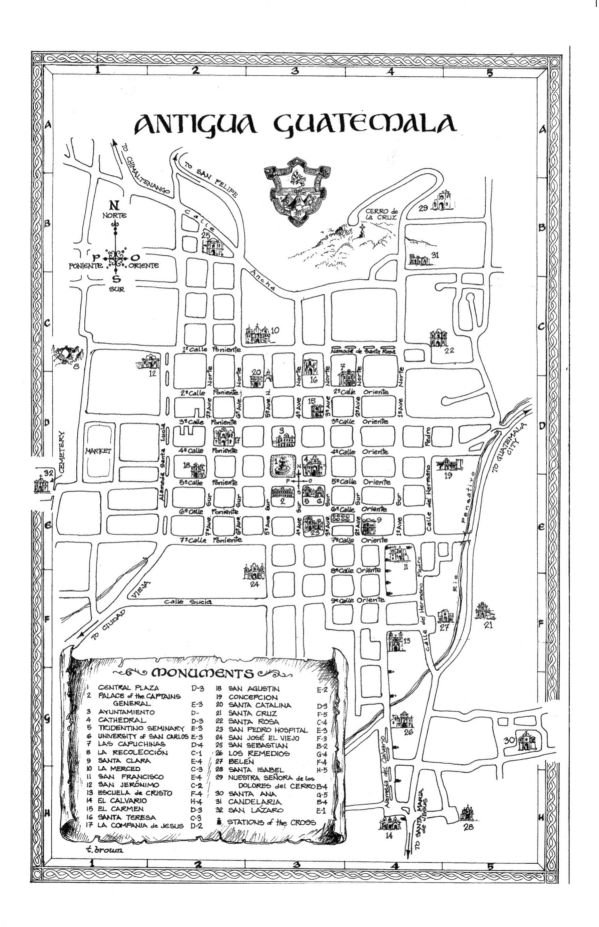

ANTIGUA GUATEMALA

MONUMENTS

#	Name	Loc	#	Name	Loc
1	CENTRAL PLAZA	D-3	18	SAN AGUSTIN	E-2
2	PALACE of the CAPTAINS GENERAL	E-3	19	CONCEPCION	D-
			20	SANTA CATALINA	D-3
3	AYUNTAMIENTO	D-	21	SANTA CRUZ	F-5
4	CATHEDRAL	D-3	22	SANTA ROSA	C-4
5	TRIDENTINO SEMINARY	E-3	23	SAN PEDRO HOSPITAL	E-3
6	UNIVERSITY of SAN CARLOS	E-3	24	SAN JOSÉ EL VIEJO	F-3
7	LAS CAPUCHINAS	D-4	25	SAN SEBASTIAN	B-2
8	LA RECOLECCIÓN	C-1	26	LOS REMEDIOS	G-4
9	SANTA CLARA	E-4	27	BELÉN	F-4
10	LA MERCED	C-3	28	SANTA ISABEL	H-5
11	SAN FRANCISCO	E-4	29	NUESTRA SEÑORA de los DOLORES del CERRO	B-4
12	SAN JERÓNIMO	C-2			
13	ESCUELA de CRISTO	F-4	30	SANTA ANA	G-5
14	EL CALVARIO	H-4	31	CANDELARIA	B-4
15	EL CARMEN	D-3	32	SAN LÁZARO	E-1
16	SANTA TERESA	C-3	✝	STATIONS of the CROSS	
17	LA COMPAÑIA de JESUS	D-2			

t. brown

SKETCHBOOK ON THE WORLD

lived in Huehuetenango for four years, then in Antigua, the former Spanish Colonial Capitol of Central America, for four years. I started my architecture and construction company restoring and renovating a large Spanish Colonial home into a school. My wife and I were married in Antigua by the mayor and it is where we started our family. I mastered pen and ink drawing and augmented my income selling drawings and maps, and illustrating books. I drew the map on the preceeding page to help students locate historic architecture in Antiqua.

The map on the next page illustrates my route of travel across Middle America sketching Mayan Ruins.

Interestingly, in Guatemala, both times my wife was pregnant, I negotiated with our doctor to deliver each baby for the price of three large framed pen and ink drawings. I retained two of the drawings from that period and they are my favorite sketches of Mayan people. One of my carpenter's beautifully crafted cedar frames for these drawings.

In 1981 when a civil war in Guatemala began to engulf us, my wife, infant daughters Jessie and Christina and I moved back to the States. Counting my time in Vietnam, I had been living in third world countries for eleven years. We loaded our meager belongings into a Chevy van which I bought for $990 and outfitted it with beds and a small stove. We traveled slowly, exploring Mayan ruins in the jungles of Guatemala, Honduras and the Yucatan Peninsula of Mexico. The drawings of Mayan ruins were completed during this trip and were published for the first time in 1988 in an American Institute of Architects New Mexico Chapter magazine titled *New*

Mexico Architecture. I was still drawing with a crow quill pen and India ink. There were times when space available to draw a particular scene was so limited I had to place the ink bottle between my feet, requiring me to bend over to dip my pen each time it needed to be recharged with ink. I sketched in the sun, wind, rain and with bugs swirling around me. We camped near the ruins and explored Copán, Quiriguá, Palenque, Chicanná, Tulum, Isla Mujeras, Chichen Itza, Mayapán, Labna, Sayil, Kabah and the massive temple complex of Uxmal.

I have had the opportunity to travel to several of these countries again. I was selected by the President of the American Institute of Architects to serve as Ambassador to the Federation of Pan American Architects Associations (FPAA). Several of the drawings in this section were made during those trips.

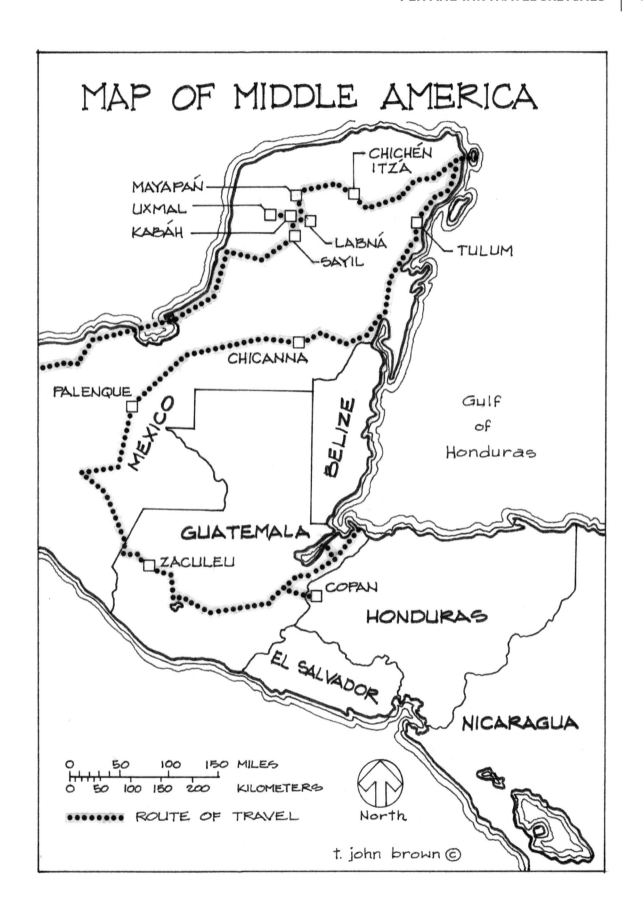

COSTA RICA

The architecture I saw on this short trip was simple and provided little historic insight, but form and detail, even on the most utilitarian buildings, are always worth sketching.

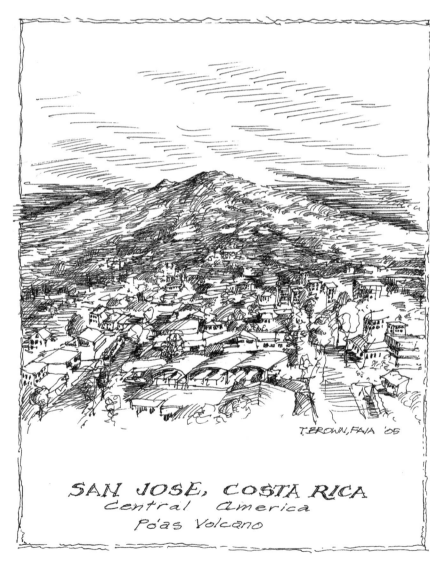

SAN JOSE, COSTA RICA
Central America
Pó'as Volcano

I drew the Corner House while drinking beer with friends in the hotel bar across the street. I wasn't particularly interested in drawing this specific house, but I was running out of time to draw anything on the trip. This view of the capital city, San Jose, was done from my hotel window. It reveals a little about the country's plain architectural style. Despite the elementary nature of the buildings, the people of San Jose made the trip worthwhile.

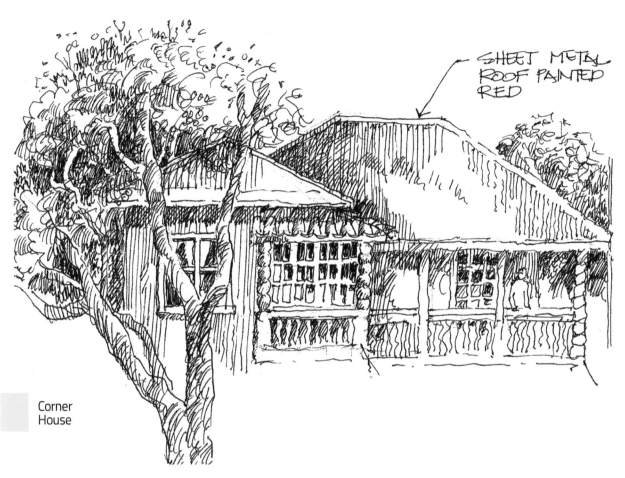

SHEET METAL
ROOF PAINTED
RED

Corner
House

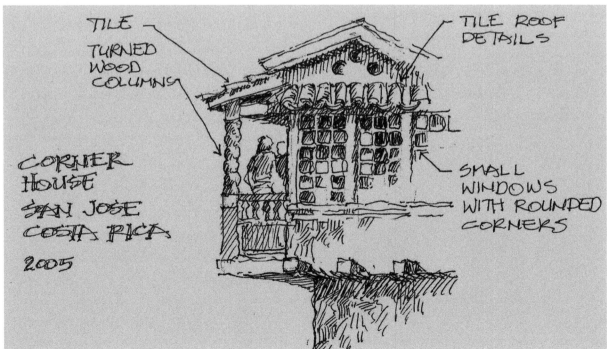

TILE

TURNED
WOOD
COLUMNS

TILE ROOF
DETAILS

CORNER
HOUSE
SAN JOSE
COSTA RICA

2005

SMALL
WINDOWS
WITH ROUNDED
CORNERS

GUATEMALA

The friendly Mayan people and their colorful weavings and dress make Guatemala a special place. Over four years I helped create linguistic centers in Antigua, Huehuetenango and Quetzaltenango in the Central Highlands and trained volunteers to work in Latin America.

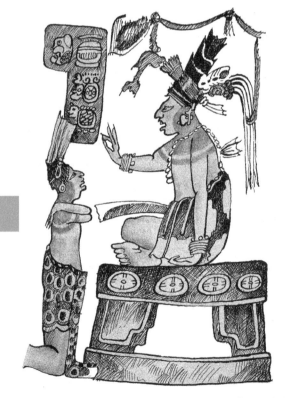

Tikal
GUATEMALA

A GUIDE TO THE MUSEUM

After serving in Vietnam, I traveled with a friend from college across Mexico and Belize to the northern jungle of Guatemala. We explored the ruins of the ancient Mayan Tikal Temple complex, and then rode a rickety bus with pigs tied to the top to Guatemala City. Eventually we arrived at the town of Antigua, a welcoming place to study the Spanish language. This historic town rests at the foot of three volcanoes and was the Spanish Colonial Capital of Central America. Antigua was abandoned in 1717 after a series of crippling earthquakes; it is now a Central American Monument. After my year and half trip across Central and South America, I returned to Antigua, where I lived for eight years. I created two language training centers in the highlands and then formed an architectural practice called Xocomil Designs.

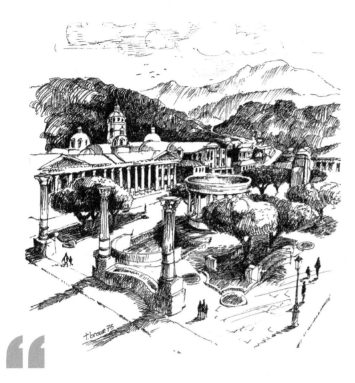

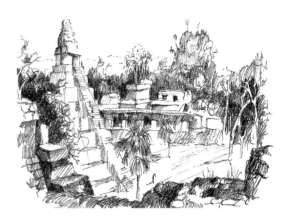

Quetzaltenango   Tikal

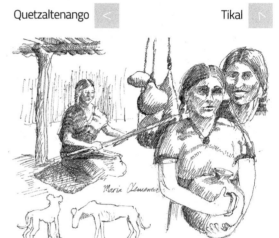

Fuente in Parque   Maria Clemensa,
Central Antigua   Antigua

"

These drawings illustrate
the area's unique mixture of
Mayan and Spanish Colonial
architecture.

Ruins of Zaculeu
-1975

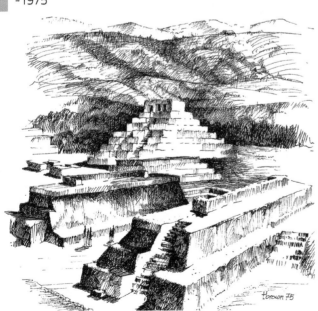

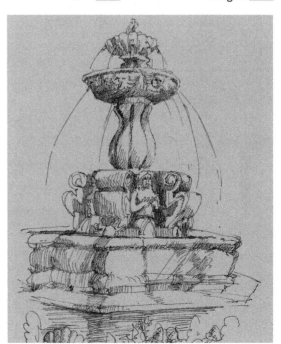

Antigua, in the Guatemalan central highlands, is famous for its well-preserved Spanish Baroque-influenced architecture and numerous colonial church ruins. It also served as the capital of the Kingdom of Guatemala.

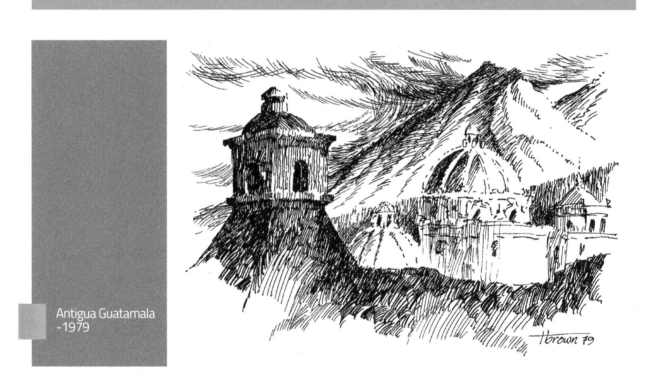

Antigua Guatamala -1979

This remarkable city was laid out in a grid, with a central square and streets running north-south and east-west. The location of church and government buildings around the central plaza underscores their significance to the community. Central Park (Parque Central) is at the city's heart. Its reconstructed fountain is a popular gathering spot. Off one side of Central Park sits the Arco de Santa Catalina, which is among the many notable architectural landmarks of "La Antigua." The entire city is surrounded by three enormous volcanoes and mountains, plains and hills and is considered to be one of the finest agricultural areas in Guatemala.

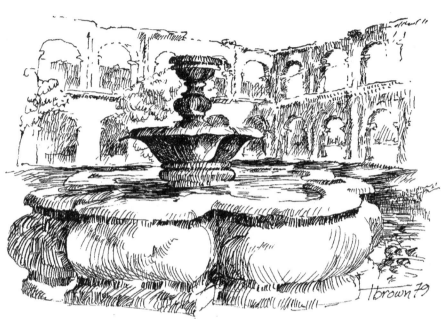

Santa Clara Cloister
Courtyard Fountain
-1979

Carved Stone
Entry-1979

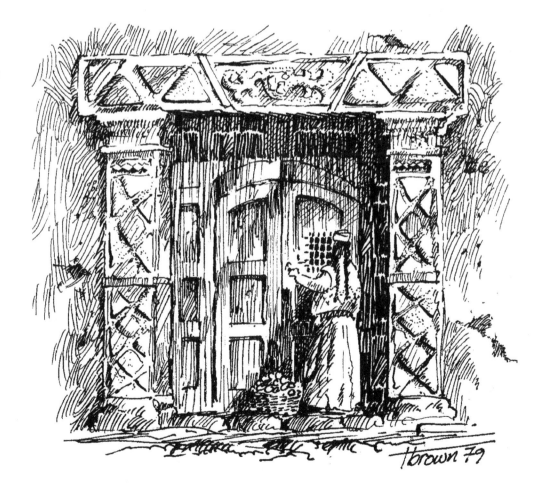

San Sabastian Church
and Volcano Aqua.
Pre-1976 Earthquake

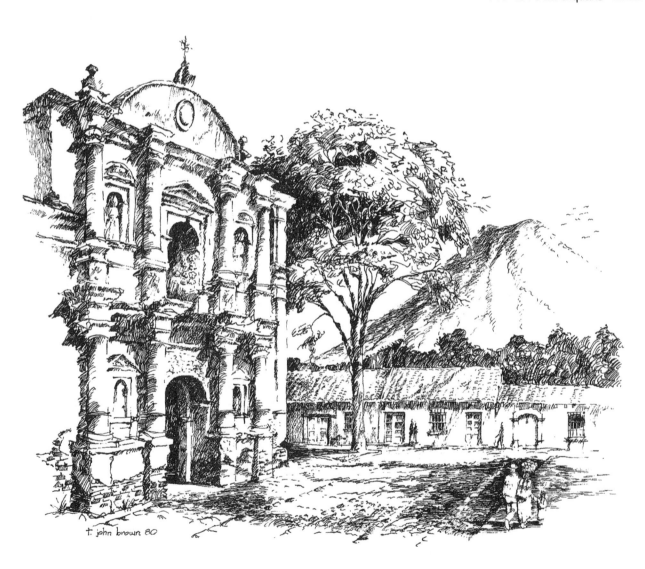

t. john brown 80

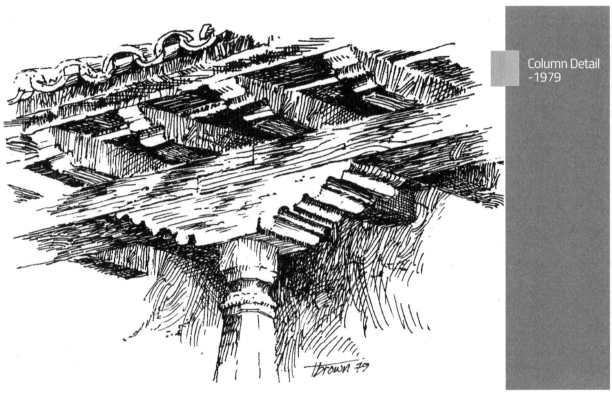

Column Detail
-1979

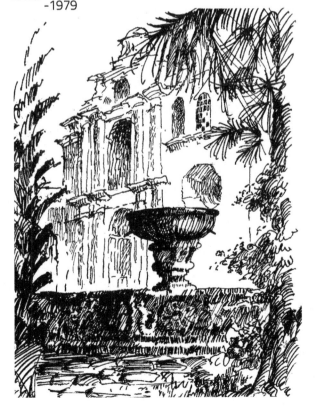

Courtyard Fountain
La Merced Church
-1979

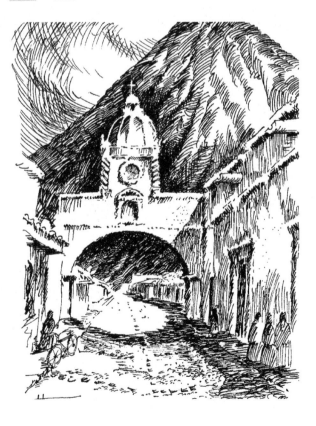

Arco de Santa Catalina
-1979

"The fragile thatched roof jungle house is as much a part of Guatemalan culture as the prominent Spanish Colonial houses of Antigua.

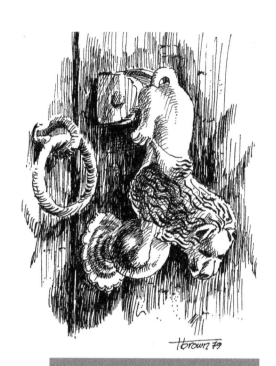

Bronze Door Knocker
-1979

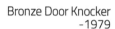

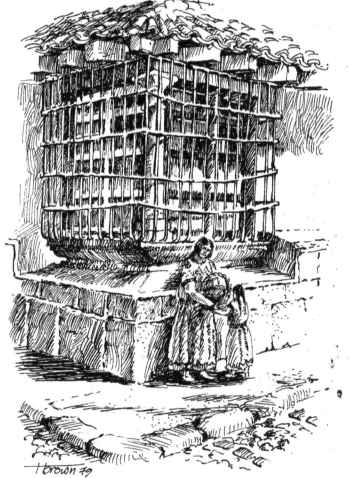

Corner Window Balcony
-1979

Rio Dulce House
-1976

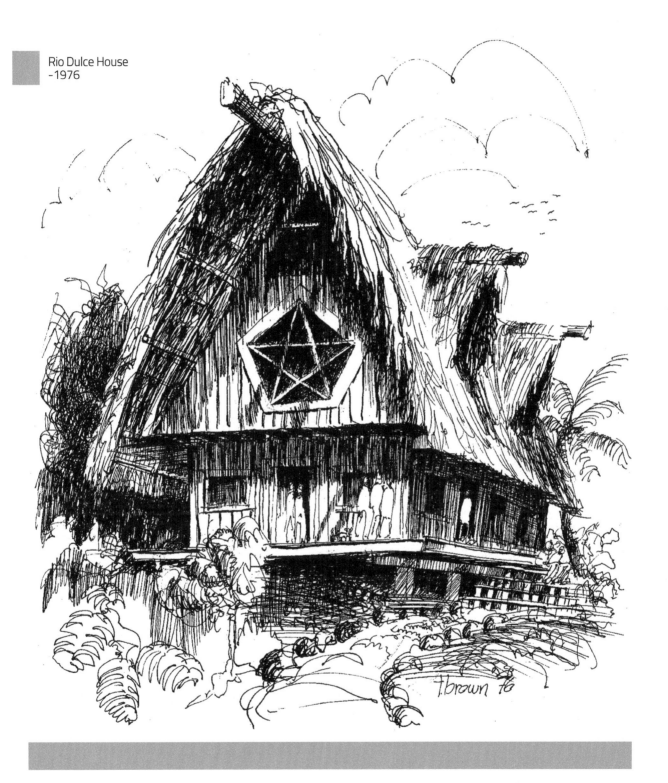

HONDURAS

Mayan ruins at Copan display some of the most intricately crafted stone monuments in Central America.

An arched opening frames this view of one of the domes of the Cathedral of Immaculate Conception in Comayagua. The sketch was completed quickly while touring the cathedral. My Honduran architect friends were so impressed with the drawing that they gave me an arched, hand-cast aluminum frame for its display. The church and market scene on the next page do not exist. I created the drawing while sitting in a long meeting.

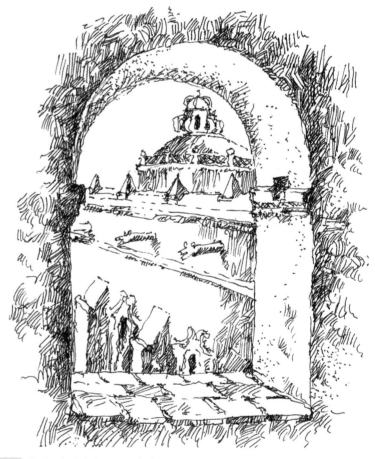

Cathedral de la Imaculada Concepcion
-2003

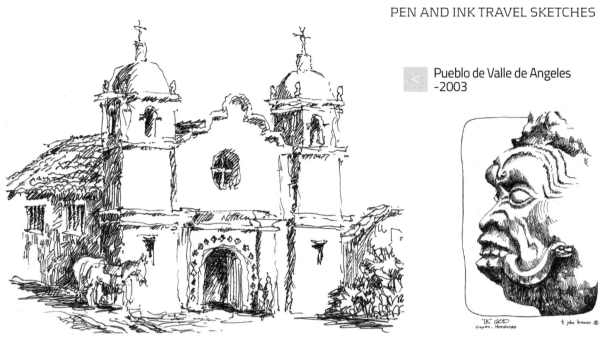

Pueblo de Valle de Angeles
-2003

"IK" GOD
Copán, Honduras

The sun radiating out to the drawing edge was an experiment
intended to focus attention on the church.

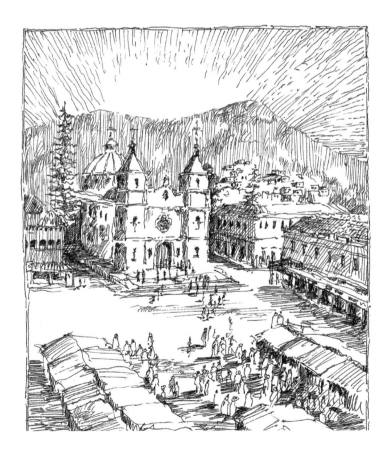

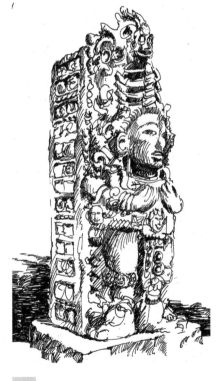

Copan Stela "A"

Honduras
-2004

MEXICO

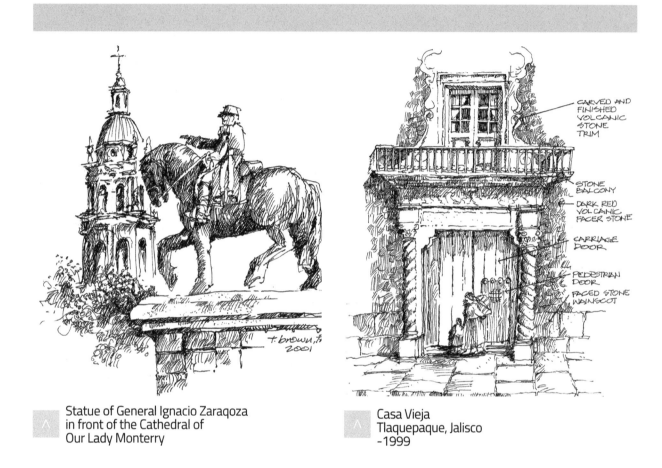

∧ Statue of General Ignacio Zaraqoza
in front of the Cathedral of
Our Lady Monterry

∧ Casa Vieja
Tlaquepaque, Jalisco
-1999

CARVED AND
FINISHED
VOLCANIC
STONE
TRIM

STONE
BALCONY

DARK RED
VOLCANIC
FACER STONE

CARRIAGE
DOOR

PEDESTRIAN
DOOR

FACED STONE
WAINSCOT

M exico was once the Spanish Colonial capital, and the history of its Spanish culture is captured in these drawings. The sketch of Casa Vieja was done late in the evening standing under a streetlight in the old part of the city called Tlaquepaque while my wife and I waited for other members of our group. The drawing of the Iglesia de la Soledad was captured while standing in the shade across the street during a tour of the old town. Many of Mexico's Aztec buildings have been leveled, but much of Aztec culture and civilization was chronicled by its Spanish conquerors. The 15 foot tall pre-Aztec warrior column from the Toltec culture is carved from basalt and once supported the roof of Quetzalcoatl's pyramid in Tula. The Toltec's occupied the Valley of Mexico around 950-1300 AD. Their warriors eventually defeated the Mayans, creating a Toltec-Mayan religion and society.

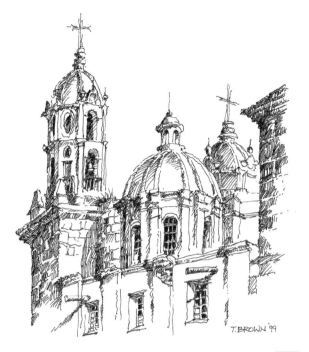

Iglesia de la Soledad
-1999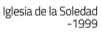

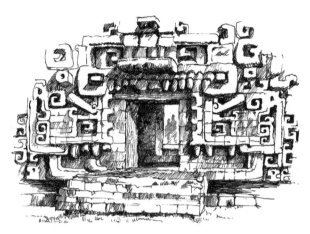

Chenes-Style Rain Monster Mask
Chicanna

> Mayan, Aztec and Spanish culture is represented by magnificent buildings and ruins throughout Mexico.

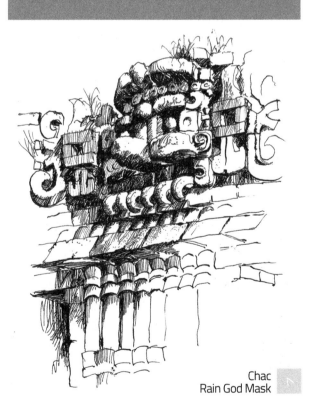

Chac
Rain God Mask

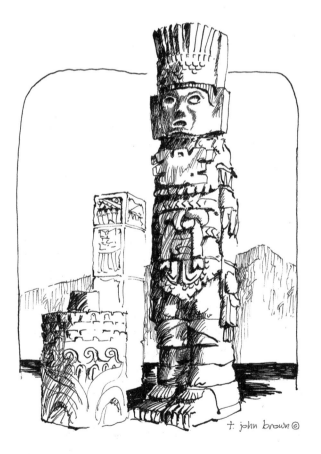

Toltec
Columns

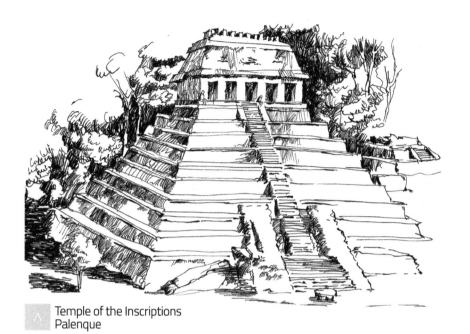
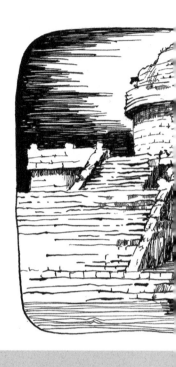

∧ Temple of the Inscriptions
Palenque

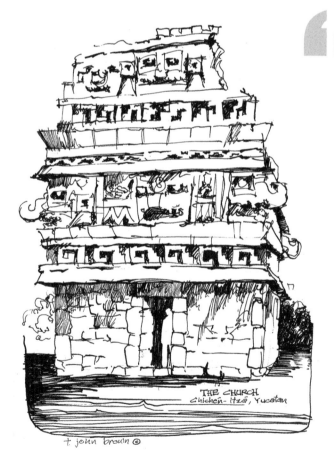

THE CHURCH
Chichen-Itza, Yucatan

† john brown ©

> "My family and I camped at every Mayan site we could find so I could draw these buildings. I had never drawn a spider, making the tarantula an especially interesting subject.

∧ The Church
Chichen Itza

> Tarantula

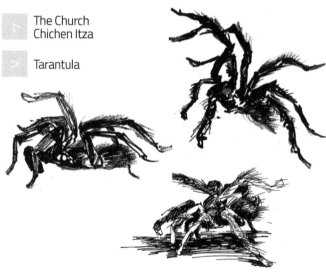

EL CARACOL
Chichén-Itzá , Yucatan

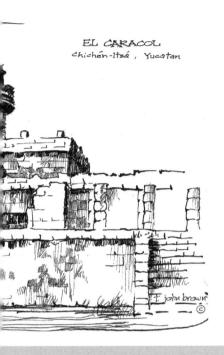

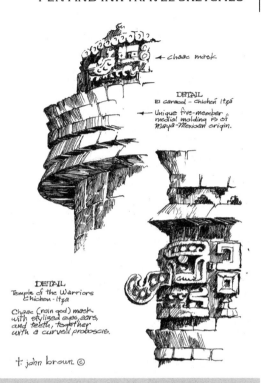

← chaac mask

DETAIL
El caracol - Chichén Itzá
← Unique five-member medial molding is of Maya-Mexican origin.

Frieze Details
Chichen Itza >

DETAIL
Temple of the Warriors
Chichen-Itza

Chaac (rain god) mask with stylised eyes, ears, and teeth, together with a curved proboscis.

t. john brown ©

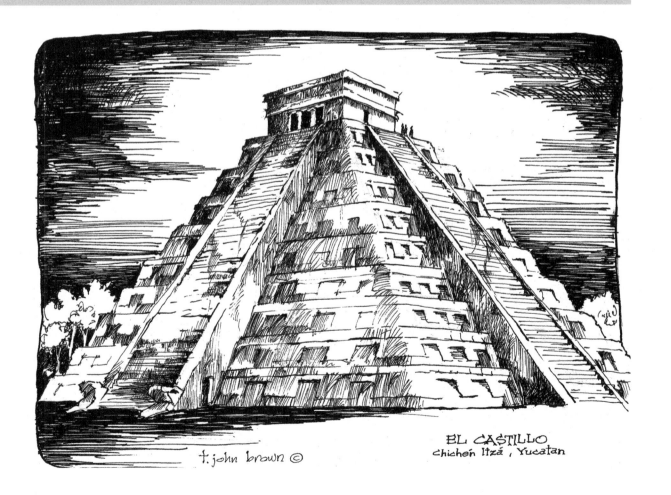

t. john brown ©

EL CASTILLO
Chichén Itzá , Yucatan

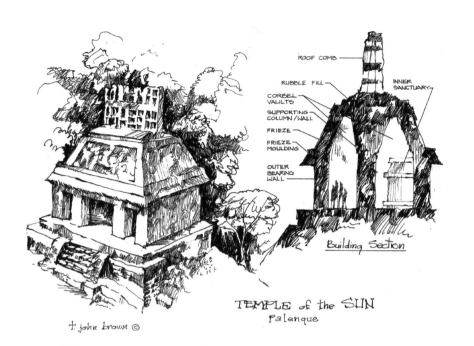

ROOF COMB

RUBBLE FILL

INNER SANCTUARY

CORBEL VAULTS

SUPPORTING COLUMN / WALL

FRIEZE

FRIEZE MOULDING

OUTER BEARING WALL

Building Section

TEMPLE of the SUN
Palenque

t. john brown ©

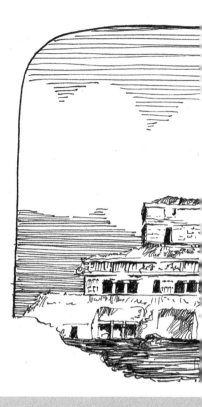

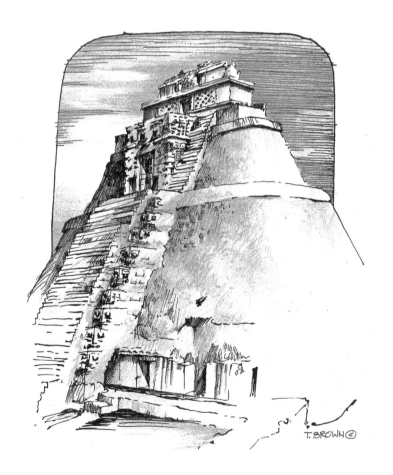

T. BROWN ©

"

The bold structure of the Pyramid of the Magician at Uxmal, pictured to the left, includes unique rounded corners; rectilinear corners are more typical in Mayan architecture.

Temple of the Magician Uxmal

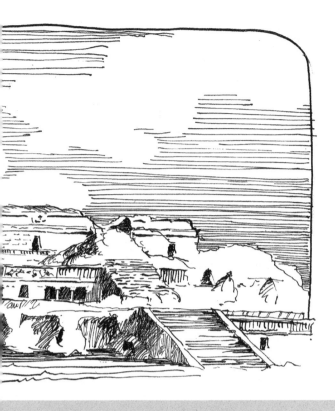

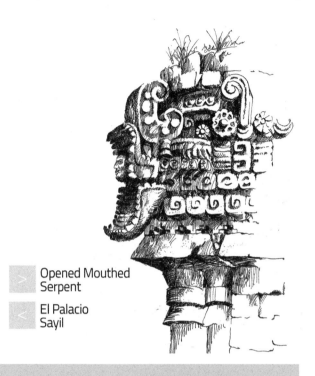

> Opened Mouthed Serpent

< El Palacio Sayil

"

The drawing at right comes from a limestone panel illustrating a Mayan ruler from Palenque named Pacal. Archeologists indicate that Palenque flourished under Pacal's rule. I use this image on my business cards.

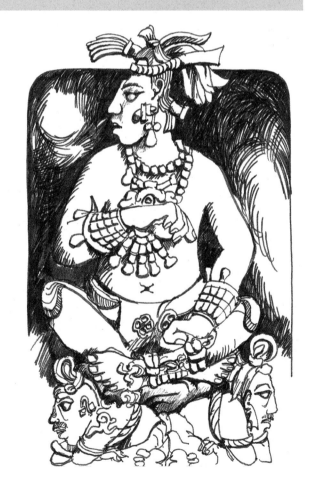

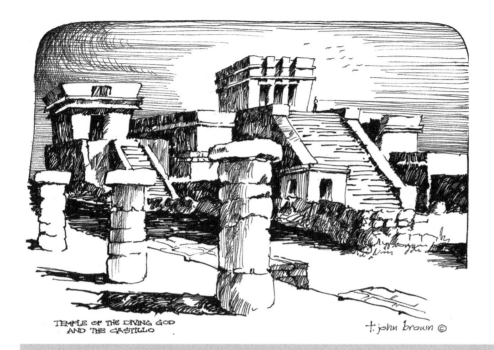

TEMPLE OF THE DIVING GOD
AND THE CASTILLO

t. john brown ©

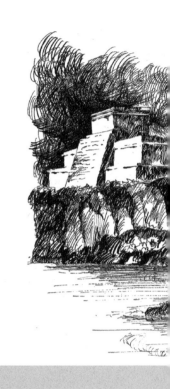

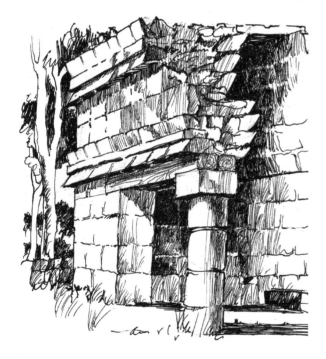

> This small building of Puuc design is without decoration except for the cornice details.
>
> The drawing at right illustrates a ceremonial gate with traditional thatched roof house forms prominently depicted on both sides of the arch.

Steam Bath
Chichen-Itza

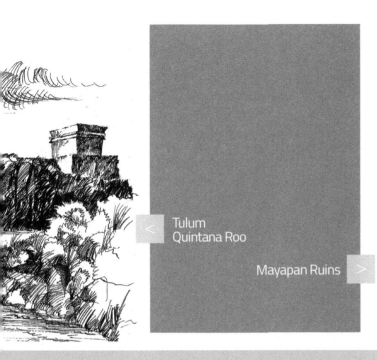

Tulum
Quintana Roo

Mayapan Ruins

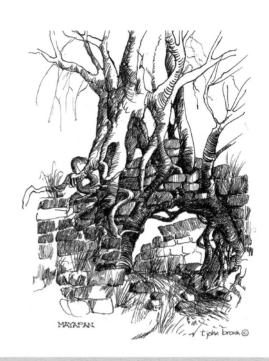

MAYAPAN
t. john brown ©

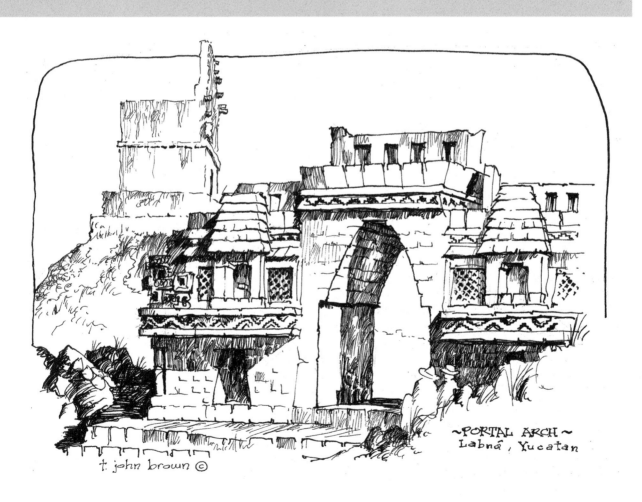

~PORTAL ARCH~
Labná, Yucatan

t. john brown ©

THE
CARIBBEAN

was fortunate to be invited to visit Puerto Rico numerous times. During my first trip, I represented the American Institute of Architects, at the international meeting of the Federation of Pan American Architect Associations. I arrived a day early to explore the massive 400-year-old battlements of Old San Juan and El Morro Fort. The iconic garitas, or sentry boxes, anchored along the edge of the heavy walls of the fort are the icons of the fort. Their distinct shape make them a perfect symbol of this important structure and for Puerto Rico itself.

For a period of fifty years after Christopher Columbus discovered the Island of Puerto Rico, Spanish ships carried plundered gold and silver from Mexico and Peru to Spain under the protection of the San Juan Forts. Spanish galleons would sail from Spain and enter to the south of Puerto Rico, dock, then sail north in the Caribbean Sea and head for Cuba and Spain with their riches.

The Caribbean Sea was a vital passageway and to protect their treasure laden sailing ships and towns, laborers built massive fortifications at significant harbors. Strategically, El Morro Fort and San Juan harbor was the Spaniard's most important harbor, their "key to the Indies." In 1595, the fort's defenders stretched a metal chain across the entrance of the bay to protect the bay from invaders. This defensive mechanism forced England's notable sailing Captain, Sir Francis Drake, to fail his attack on El Morro.

My first trip to the Caribbean was in 1980, while I was living in Guatemala. A major hurricane tore across several Caribbean Islands damaging buildings in its path. My colleague, Bob Gersony and I, were contracted by the US Agency for International Development to survey and provide a hurricane damage assessment of every public building on the island of St. Lucia. Our report included my quickly drawn illustrations of the damaged buildings and provided recommendations on improving and strengthening structural systems for Caribbean Island communities.

Another member of our team was a structural engineer from Barbados who, before flying to St. Lucia, treated us to an appetizing lunch at a men's club in the capitol of Bridgetown. The wood paneled interior and nattily dressed men sitting in large leather covered sofas reminded me of turn of the century British décor during a period when England occupied land around the world. The large dining room tables were covered with white linen and women dressed in pressed white dresses attended us. When we were escorted to our table, it was interesting to find a broad array of formal silverware settings placed around the plates, appearing as so many ships blockading an island.

My wife traveled with me to the Island of Guadeloupe, a French overseas territory located several Caribbean Islands north of St. Lucia. I was invited to attend the FPAA Congress of Architects representing the architects of the Americas. We sat

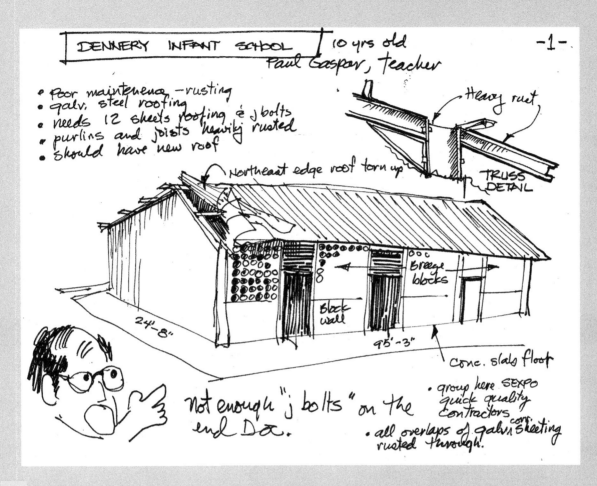

St. Lucia hurricane damage

in meetings for two days. All night long we heard the ubiquitous chirping of tiny frogs through the slatted windows. During the meetings, we were provided with earphones to tune into any of three languages; Spanish, French and English. Women sitting in booth's in the back of the meeting room provided the translations. Several architects from Latin American countries, to include one from Cuba, ran for President, but my compatriot Gabriel Durand Hollis, FAIA, was elected FPAA President and I was elected, North American Secretary for four year terms.

Due to time constraints, there were no tours to visit the island or even its capitol. Between meetings, I had to settle on sketching the swimming pool and people's faces. Look at how I drew the curly hair of the fellow in the lower right of the group.

I sketched a photograph of a Guadeloupe country house to help me remember the architectural flavor of this island. Ubiquitous Spanish tile roofs were typical of country homes and slats covering windows allowed trade winds to cool off the interiors.

PUERTO RICO

This small island is aptly named Puerto Rico (Rich Port) for its Spanish Colonial history, stories of pirate attacks and warm days under arching palm trees.

During my first of four trips to Puerto Rico, I arrived in San Juan a day early so I could spend a day at Old San Juan and El Morro, the Spanish Colonial fort designed to guard the entrance to San Juan Bay. The Water Battery, at the bottom of the main artillery ramp, is so close to sea level that its cannon could damage the hulls of enemy ships. At this site gunners actually engaged the British ships of Sir Francis Drake in 1595. The sentry boxes (garitas) located along the outer edges of the fortification wall are iconic symbols of the fort and often used as such for Puerto Rico. At the luxurious Caribe Hilton Hotel, I took the opportunity to sketch the stand of palm trees that surrounded its scenic pool.

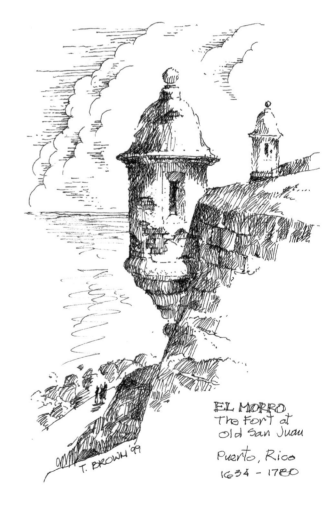

EL MORRO
The Fort at
Old San Juan
Puerto, Rico
1634 - 1780

T. BROWN '09

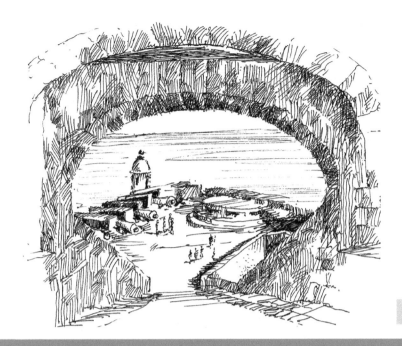

El Morro Artillery Ramp
-1999

Beach at the Caribe
Hilton - San Juan
- 2001

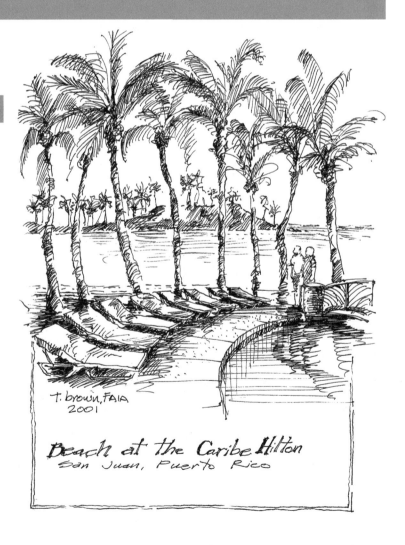

WEST INDIES

"

I always try to draw something where ever I travel, even if it is the hotel swimming pool. The Traveller's Palm Tree was fun to add to the drawing; then I returned home to learn about them.

Creole Beach Hotel
-2004

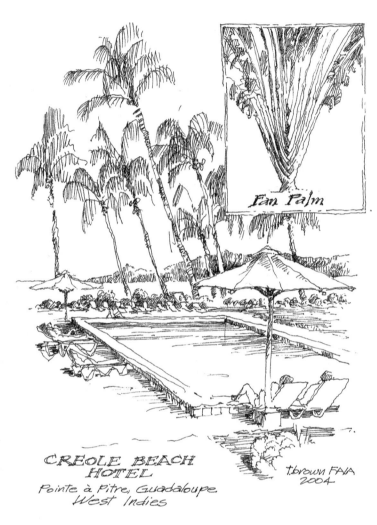

Fan Palm

CREOLE BEACH HOTEL
Pointe à Pitre, Guadeloupe.
West Indies

t.brown FAIA
2004

My wife and I visitied the Island of Guadeloupe for the 22nd Pan American Congress of Architects, where I was elected to serve as the North American Secretary for 4 years. Guadeloupe was discovered by Christopher Columbus in 1493 and made a French Overseas Department in 1946 and a French Region in 1974. This was our first experience using the new European currency, the Euro. I sketched faces of Congress attendees and made a quick drawing of the hotel swimming pool and the Traveler Palm Tree, or Ravenala, which is not a palm, but a member of the plant family Strelitziaceae from Madagascar and similar to Bird of Paradise and banana plants.

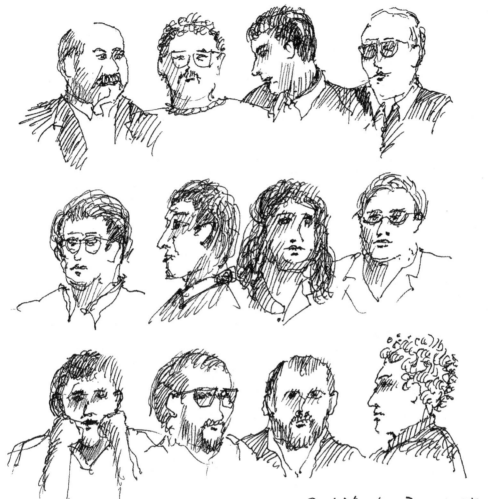

Members of the Pan American Architects Association
Guadeloupe, West Indies

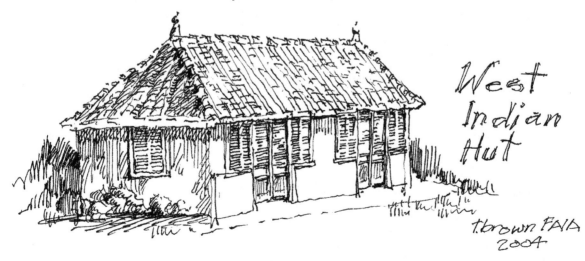

West
Indian
Hut

t.brown FAIA
2004

NORTH
AMERICA

Over the years, I traveled for my architectural work to far flung places on the sprawling Navajo Nation in New Mexico and Arizona and to various Indian Reservations in Montana, Washington, Idaho, North Dakota and South Dakota. I also traveled across the USA, from New York to California and from Florida to Wisconsin and places in between. Some of my favorite sketches remind me of multiple visits to Washington DC while attending meetings with the American Institute of Architects. The iconic Octagon House, and temporary home of U.S. President James Madison and his wife Dolly, is where they lived after the British burned the White House. The U.S. Capitol Dome is found in several of my drawing and it should be noted that you do not have to draw the entire building to capture the essence of its strength.

My work training architects to assist people get back in their homes after disasters took me to the Provinces of British Columbia, Saskatchewan, and Nova Scotia, Canada. I always try to find time to make at least one drawing, even if it is just a quick sketch, to capture a memory of that trip. It is not unusual for me to begin a sketch and complete it later.

My wife and several friends rode trustworthy mules to the bottom of the Grand Canyon. The next day, I hiked along the river bottom to one of the two bridges across the Colorado River and sketched the iconic geologic formation high above the river called Mexican Hat. Notice the mules with riders on the right plodding along on the same trail we rode down on. While in Arizona, touring Frank Lloyd Wright's Taliesin West, I decided to capture a portion of his iconic studio and Winter home and how this famous architect exposed large stones as elements of design in concrete walls.

Boat scenes are fun to draw and can be done effectively with squiggly, unexacting lines. The masts, and jumble of boat hulls and water dazzle the eye. I encourage you to try your hand at drawing boats tied to a dock. You can see this in one of the drawing from California. In Florida, I framed the Renaissance Vinoy Resort Hotel tower in St. Petersburg, Florida with the sailboat masts and cable supports. I positioned myself at this vantage point to focus this drawing on the tower. Palm trees can also be fun to draw and are not that difficult, but you should be careful to give three-dimensional depth to the palms or the palm fronds will appear flat.

Two of the drawings I did in Savannah, Georgia were done while I was strolling around the city center with a friend. We were looking for a good place to eat and I wanted to sketch a couple of buildings but I had to do it while my friend was with me. So, I hurried through the drawing which, because I drew them rapidly, have a life of their own due to the squiggly lines. We just exited the Chart House Restaurant and I thought the entrance door and adjacent window of the brick building would make a good drawing.

Hawaii was a treat and drawing the little pineapple at the Dole Plantation was fun. It did not take much time and left me with a wonderful memory of Hawaii. Doing a drawing of the USS Arizona Memorial was difficult because this monument evoked deep emotions. The small memorial bridges the sunken ship where so many men died during the attack on Pearl Harbor. I decided to sketch people looking out of one of the openings facing the USS Missouri which ironically, is docked nearby. It was on that ship where Japan surrendered, ending World War II. As I toured the USS Missouri I decided that a sketch of the giant guns would be a fitting record of this great battle ship.

I enjoyed having the time to sketch the Corinthian column capitols in the Idaho State Capitol building. This sort of drawing takes a lot of time but can be worth the effort. The drawings in Illinois were focused in Chicago because I spent several days attending The American Institute of Architects national convention. The historic arch that Louis Sullivan designed was interesting to me because this was a detail that I was required to include as an entry gateway to the design I did for my architectural license exam. The Robie House, an iconic house designed by Frank Lloyd Wright in the Prairie School style, is considered by many to be the uniquely American style of design. The projecting cantilevered roof eaves and brick bands emphasized the horizontal, reminding Wright of the American prairie.

I greatly enjoyed doing the two Montana drawings. One was sketched in my home town of Hardin where I grew up and the other at the nearby Battle of the Little Bighorn National Monument. Even as a boy, without much knowledge of our government's policy of trying to eradicate Native Americans, I was more impressed with the success of the Sioux and Cheyenne Indians and their overwhelming force that wiped out General Colonel George Armstrong Custer and his men who attacked their camp.

Las Vegas, Nevada is a unique and fun place to visit and the Venetian Casino Hotel was interesting, with its replication of architectural elements of

Venice, Italy. I visited Venice as a young man and enjoyed the illusion of these icons. Outside of Las Vegas, is Lake Tahoe, a stunningly beautiful clear lake on the border of California. Nearby, the ill-fated Donner Party, a group of people in a wagon train to California in 1846, were snowbound in the Sierra Nevada Mountains. Some of the pioneers resorted to cannibalism to survive.

> The only way to improve drawing horses is to practice.

I appreciated the famous architect, Michael Graves, FAIA opening his home for the Board of Directors of the American Institute of Architects for a backyard party and tour of his iconic home. I enjoyed being able to sketch elements of Princeton University and as always, had to take available moments to draw while on tour. Drawing the lion head table braces and the iconic roof cupola was all I needed to capture the character of this campus.

Because I live and work in New Mexico, I have plenty of opportunity to draw as I travel around this state. I try to capture the scenes whether in Santa Fe, or touring historic churches. Pueblo Revival style buildings are fun to draw and are reminiscent of early Native American adobe buildings and homes scattered in numerous pueblos across the state. I particularly enjoy the scene of Taos Pueblo and the pueblo fire place that is characteristically built in the corner of pueblo homes and decorated with brown earth tone colors.

The only way I know of how to improve drawing horses is to practice. It is best to begin drawing horses in a stall or while they are standing in a corral. Pay attention to their defined muscles and capture those details in your drawing. Simple crosshatching will help express these elements. The position of horse's ears is one of the ways horses express themselves. When their ears are pinned back, they are angry. When they are interested in something their ears swivel forward. When they are relaxed their ears flop down and indicates they are resting.

The giant pit in New York City called Ground Zero, where the World Trade Center skyscrapers were attacked, killing 2,977 victims was as heart wrenching to see as the Oklahoma City National Memorial where 168 adults and children died by the hands of terrorists. Of course, the Alamo in San Antonio, Texas where brave men died fighting a vast Mexican Army was just as emotional. These types of drawings can invoke strong memories of your visit.

Another Frank Lloyd Wright structure that caught my eye was a small, uniquely shaped windmill and water tower on the grounds of Taliesin East, Wright's sprawling home and studio in Wisconsin. Instead of being overwhelmed trying to figure out what to draw while visiting this large home, I focused on this small windmill and came home with a good memory of this farm. Drawing small focused scenes can provide you with an excellent memory.

Even though I grew up near Yellowstone Park, I never had the opportunity to visit Old Faithful geyser or Old Faithful Inn until I was grown and a full-fledged architect. What struck me as I wandered through the immense historic lodge, was how vast the interior space was. This huge volume was supported by spindly, twisted and deformed log columns and beams. I decided to lay out six square boxes on a single page of my sketchbook and draw small sketches of portions of the building. That way, I could capture numerous details with simple lines. The small size of the individual drawings make this a fun way to draw details.

Drawing people can be a challenge. So many times, over the years, I have found myself sitting in meetings trying to draw the heads and faces of people, many of them friends. Drawing heads and shoulders, especially while people are sitting, makes drawing them a lot easier.

ARIZONA

My wife and I rode mules to the bottom of the Grand Canyon and stayed for two nights at Phantom Ranch along the Colorado River. We thankfully rode those same mules back to the top.

H iking, rafting the Colorado River and riding mule-back in the Grand Canyon are all part of the Arizona experience. The 1,000 year old White House Ruin cliff dwelling, high above Chinle Wash at Canyon de Chelly National Monument, and the iconic work of Frank Lloyd Wright's Taliesin West both exhibit the rich diversity of Arizona's culture and architecture. I traveled hundreds of miles across Arizona touring and designing educational, and healthcare facilities and housing for the people of the Navajo Nation, Hualapai and Gila River Tribes. The "arms" on the Saguaro cactus indicate that this giant is at least 75 years old; it will likely live another hundred years or more.

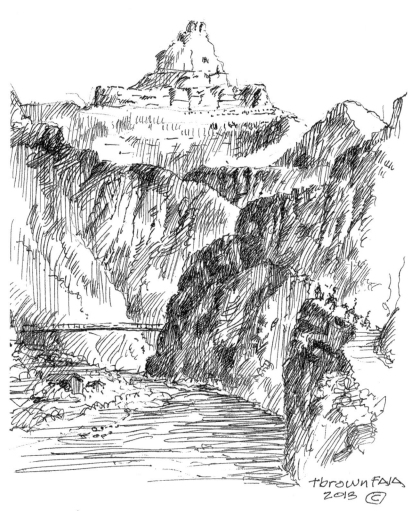

tbrownFAIA
2013 ©

GRAND CANYON
Mexican Hat, Black Bridge and Colorado River

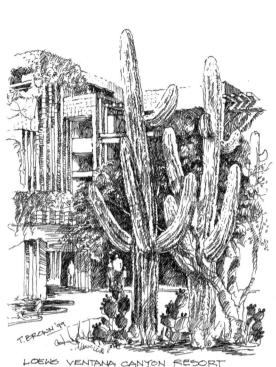

LOEWS VENTANA CANYON RESORT
TUCSON, ARIZONA

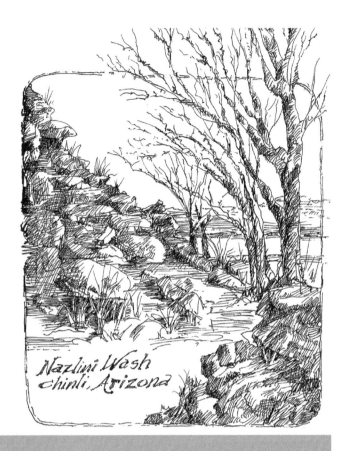

Nazlini Wash
chinli, Arizona

San Xavier del Bac Mission
~2009

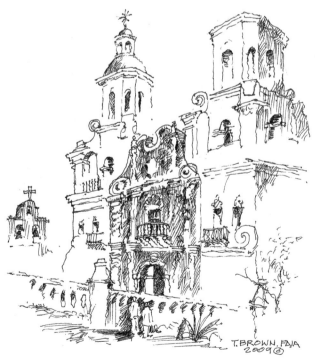

"

The Navajo Hogan reflects one of the most important cultural elements of the tribe. The door always faces east to greet "the new day and the rising sun."

Navajo Hogan

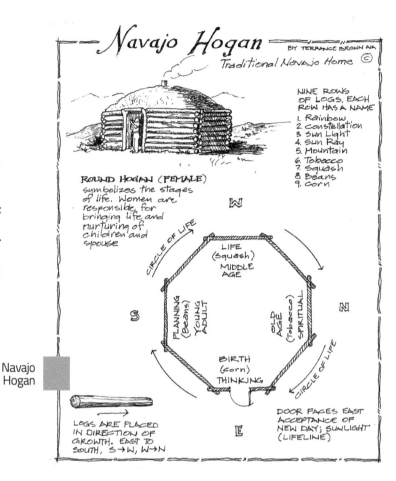

White House Ruins
Canyon de Chelly

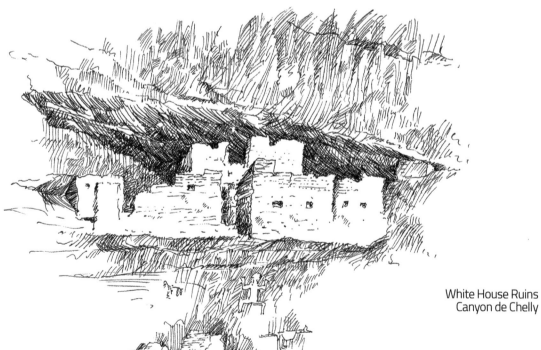

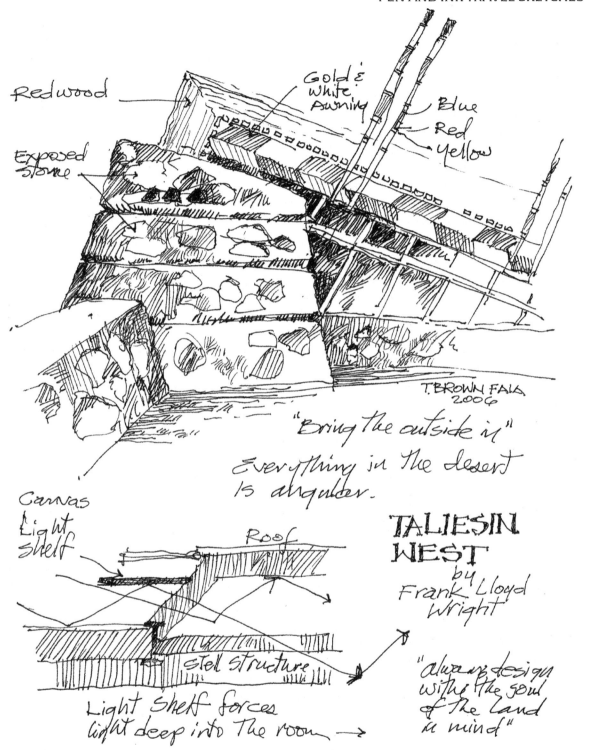

Redwood

Gold & White Awning

Blue
Red
Yellow

Exposed Stone

T. BROWN FAIA
2006

"Bring the outside in"

Everything in the desert is angular.

Canvas
Light Shelf

Roof

Steel Structure

TALIESIN WEST
by Frank Lloyd Wright

Light Shelf forces light deep into The room →

"always design with the soul of the land in mind"

CALIFORNIA

Downtown San Francisco is exceptionally walkable, and people naturally gravitate to the unique culture and food of Chinatown. The Pacific Ocean and diverse types of watercraft make great drawing subjects in places like San Diego.

The Chinatown Gate was sketched from my San Francisco hotel widow. The street behind the gate sloped up, making an unusual single point perspective. High contrast linework helps define roof lines and tiles. Nearby, I sketched Frank Lloyd Wright's Circle Gallery and included a tortured tree in the drawing's foreground. I love the lighting detail that Wright included in the wall pattern.

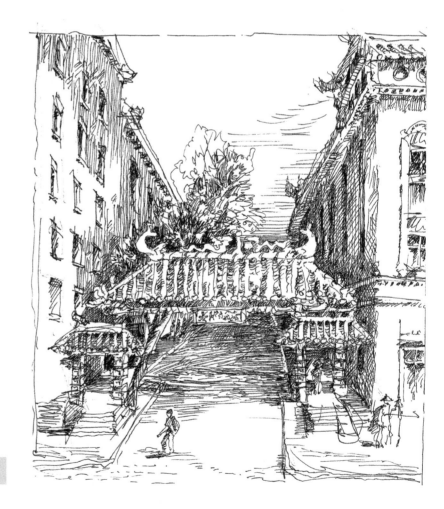

China Town Gate -2005

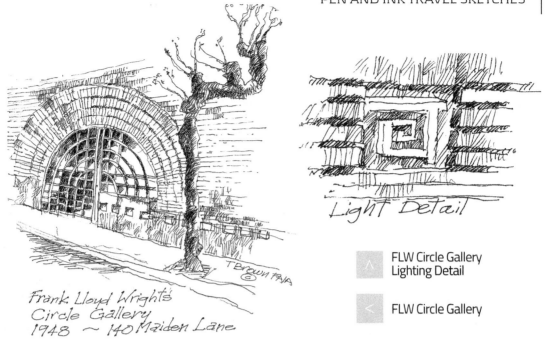

Frank Lloyd Wright's
Circle Gallery
1948 ~ 140 Maiden Lane.

FLW Circle Gallery
Lighting Detail

FLW Circle Gallery

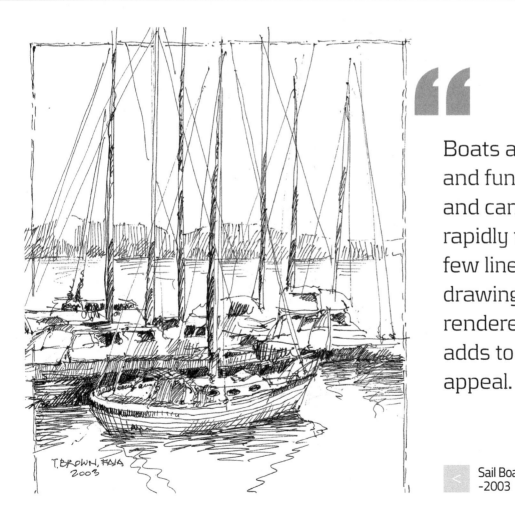

"

Boats are easy and fun to draw and can be done rapidly with a few lines. This drawing is loosely rendered, which adds to its visual appeal.

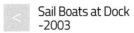

Sail Boats at Dock
-2003

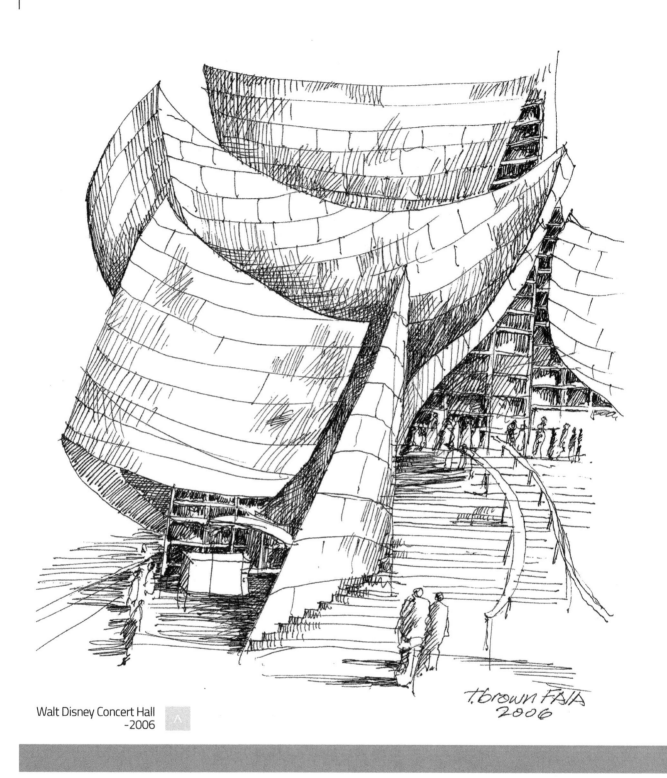

Walt Disney Concert Hall
-2006

t.brown FAIA
2006

Frank Gehry's Disney Concert Hall in downtown Los Angeles is unlike any building I have seen before and was a riot to draw. The zinc metal skin is actually a scrim, raised on metal tabs. The auditorium's curving masses and organ pipes, which appeared like "pickup sticks," were a sketching challenge.

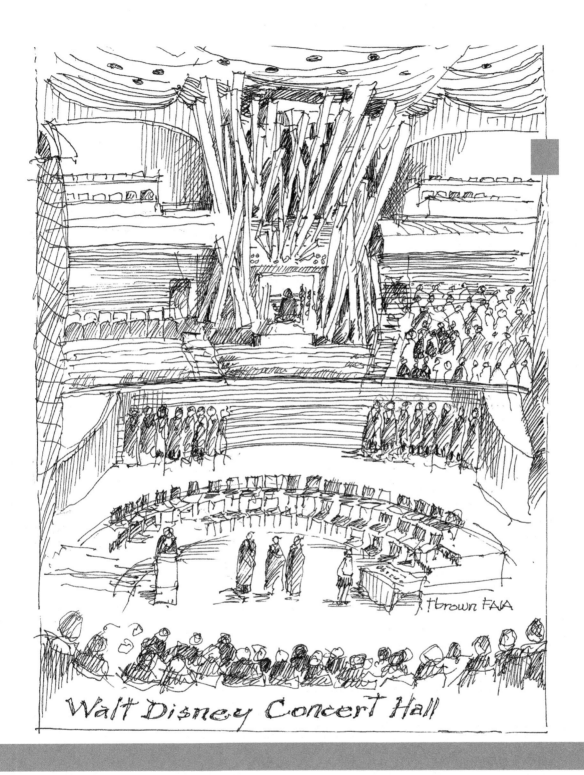

Walt Disney Concert Hall

CANADA

"

Drawing the unique architecture and character of a new place while traveling can add excitement and depth to your portfolio.

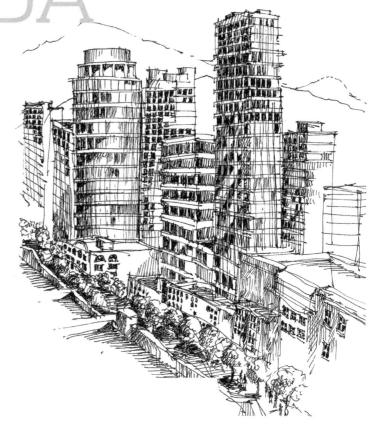

Downtown Vancouver ›

Fairmont Hotel Vancouver -2007 ↘

The steep roofline of Vancouver's Fairmont Hotel makes a bold architectural statement and an intriguing drawing project. The small dormer windows look like peering eyes. The view of high rise buildings, sketched from my hotel window, is notable in that tall buildings line one side of the street and older, truncated, masonry buildings line the other.

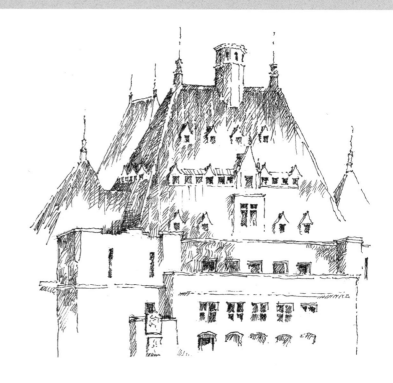

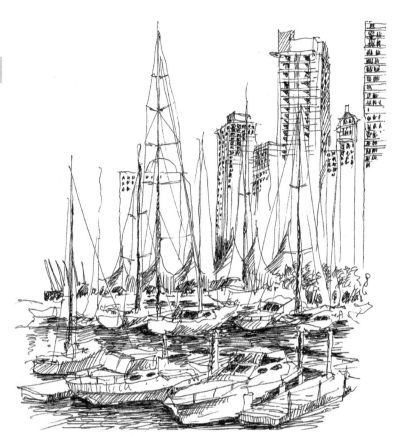

Vancouver Harbour
-2006

As I walked along the water's edge searching for something to draw in Fredericton, New Brunswick, I was attracted to the unsual shape and material of this lighthouse. Its all wood structure is clad in white painted siding. Nearby, the Gothic Revival style Christ Church Cathedral, built 1845 to 1853, is relatively small.

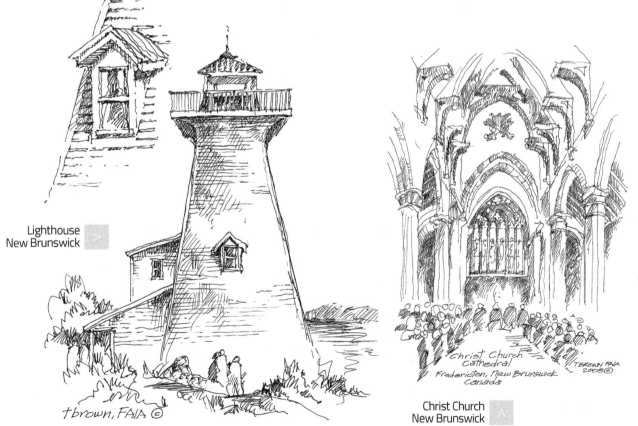

Lighthouse
New Brunswick

t brown, FAIA ©

Christ Church
Cathedral
Fredericton, New Brunswick
Canada

TBROWN FAIA
2008©

Christ Church
New Brunswick

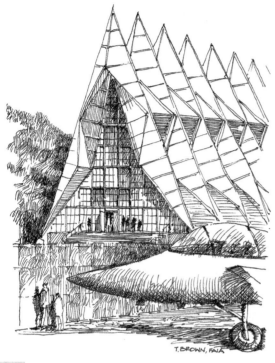

USAF Chapel

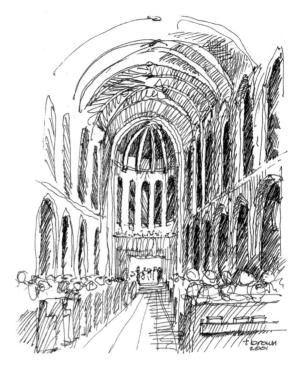

St. Johns Cathedral
-2001

COLORADO

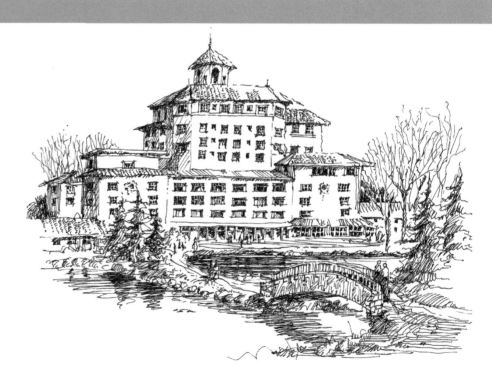

The Broadmore Hotel

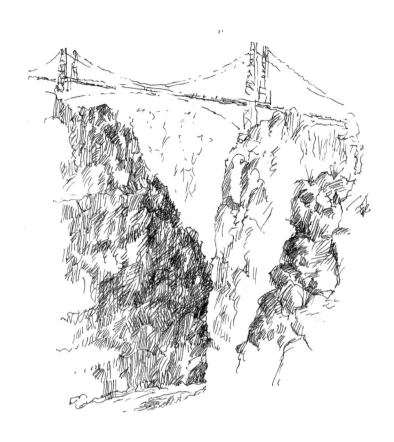

"The bridge across Royal Gorge, the Air Force Academy and its chapel, and the Broadmore Hotel are all unique to Colorado. The Academy is the newest military academy in the US and graduated its first class in 1959.

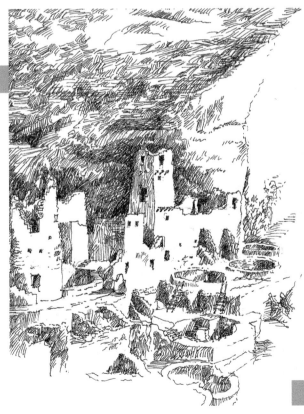

The cliff dwelling at Mesa Verde National Monument was a difficult drawing due to the broad, heavy, dark sandstone ceiling above the complex. The circular elements are the remains of underground ceremonial and religious spaces called Kiva's. Ancient Native American's used heavy logs to support the roof structures, followed by a layer of latillas (smaller tree branches) and clay. Entry to the buildings was normally by pole ladders from a roof opening, which offered protection from attack. The ladders were simply pulled up if needed.

Mesa Verde Cliff Dwelling
-2005

FLORIDA

Visiting Florida for the first time, I escorted a group of US Peace Corp Volunteers from Miami to Guatemala. I accompanied one of the volunteers to a store in Miami, where I surprised him by bartering for a pocket knife. He was amazed one can barter in the States.

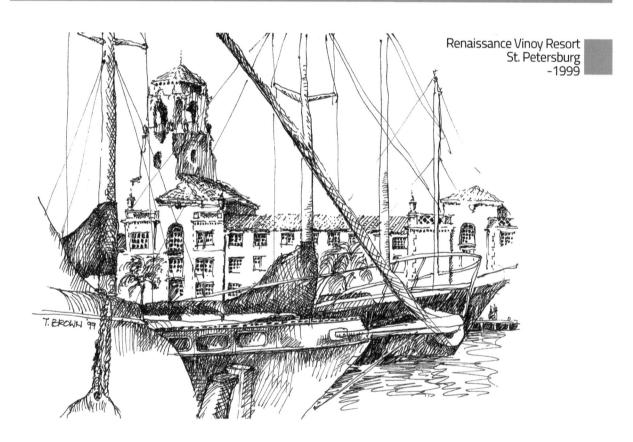

Renaissance Vinoy Resort
St. Petersburg
-1999

After arriving in Tampa I was immediately attracted to the Hotel Vinoy's boat dock and spent considerable time drawing this complex scene. The juxtaposition of the hotel, the boat masts and stay lines intrigued me.

The nearby crisscross palm frond pattern on the tree trunk against the masonry Bath House is remarkable. The Spanish tile roof with its cupola and brick detailing made for a nice detail sketch to remember Tampa.

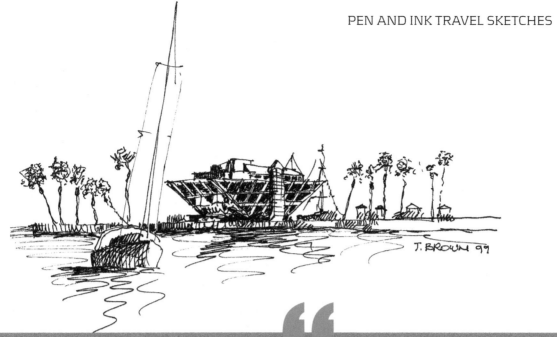

T. BROWN 99

The Pier
-1999   ∧

Matheson Hammock Park
-2000   ∨

Bath House
-1999   ∨

" Palm Trees are a welcome change from drawing the detail of broad leaf trees.

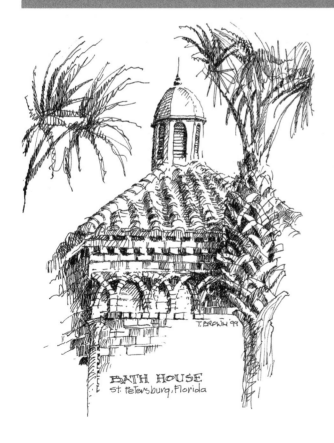

T. BROWN 99

BATH HOUSE
St. Petersburg, Florida

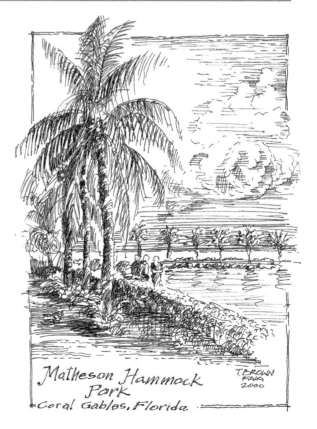

T. BROWN
FAIA
2000

Matheson Hammock
Park
Coral Gables, Florida

GEORGIA

A very loose, squiggly drawing style adds tremendous unintended interest to a composition.

One afternoon my friends and I decided to go fishing on a resort lake. I put my line in the water, but the weather was too hot and muggy to just sit in the boat gripping a fishing pole. Sketching a scene of my friend's boat was much more interesting, but keeping my sketchbook dry was a challenge. The two other drawings in Savannah were sketched loosely because I was in a hurry.

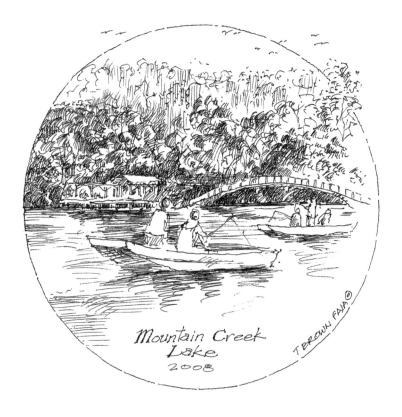

Mountain Creek Lake
-2008

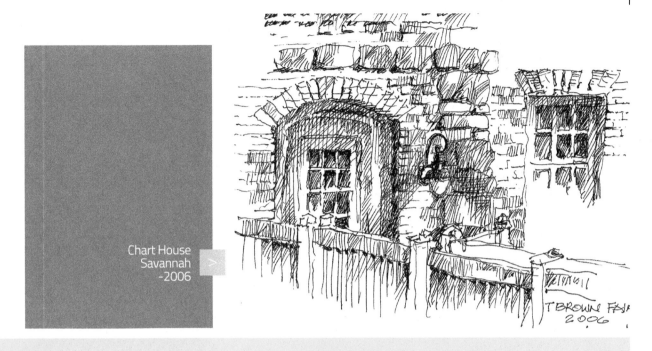

Chart House
Savannah
-2006 >

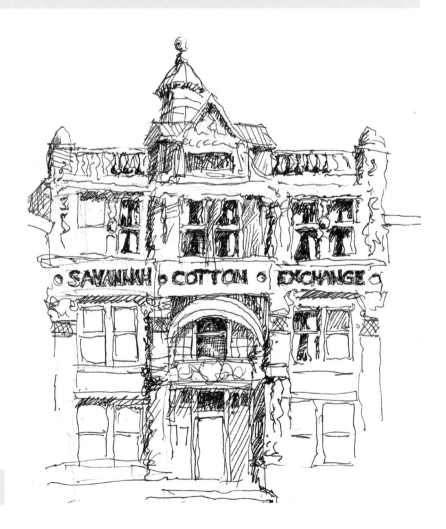

"

A loose sketch
drawn quickly
with wavy lines
develops a
special character
all its own.

Savannah Cotton Exchange
-2006

HAWAII

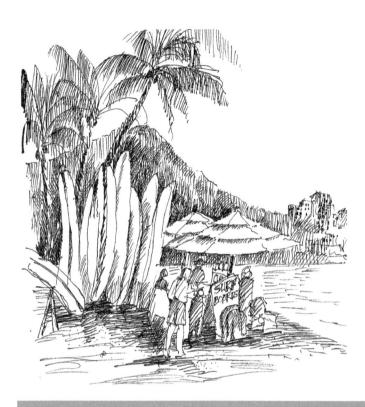

The drive around
the main island
of Oahu took less
than a day, leaving
time for lunch
along North Beach
and a sketch of a
pineapple plant.

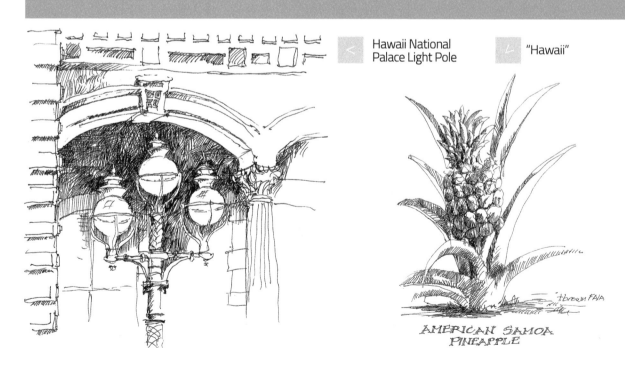

‹ Hawaii National
Palace Light Pole

∟ "Hawaii"

AMERICAN SAMOA
PINEAPPLE

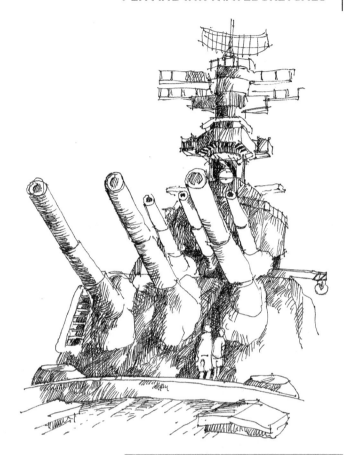

Stepping from the boat onto the USS Arizona Memorial, which straddles the World War II sunken battle ship, was a touching experience. The USS Arizona was attacked by the Japanese on December 7, 1941, killing 1,177 sailors. The USS Missouri is moored nearby on Ford Island. Japan surrendered to General MacArthur on that battleship's deck, ending the war in the Pacific Theater nearly four years later, on September 2, 1945.

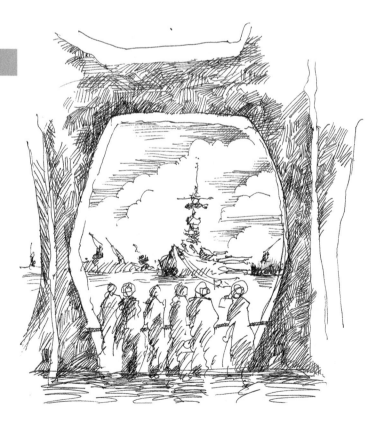

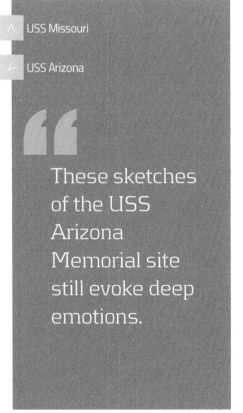

∧ USS Missouri

∠ USS Arizona

"These sketches of the USS Arizona Memorial site still evoke deep emotions.

IDAHO

Practice drawing Greek corinthian columns really pays off when you want to draw a curving colonnade that is loaded with detail.

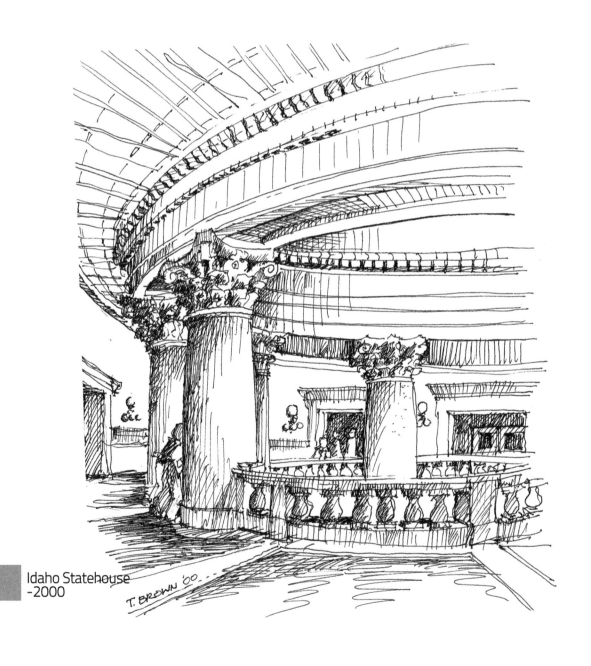

Idaho Statehouse
-2000

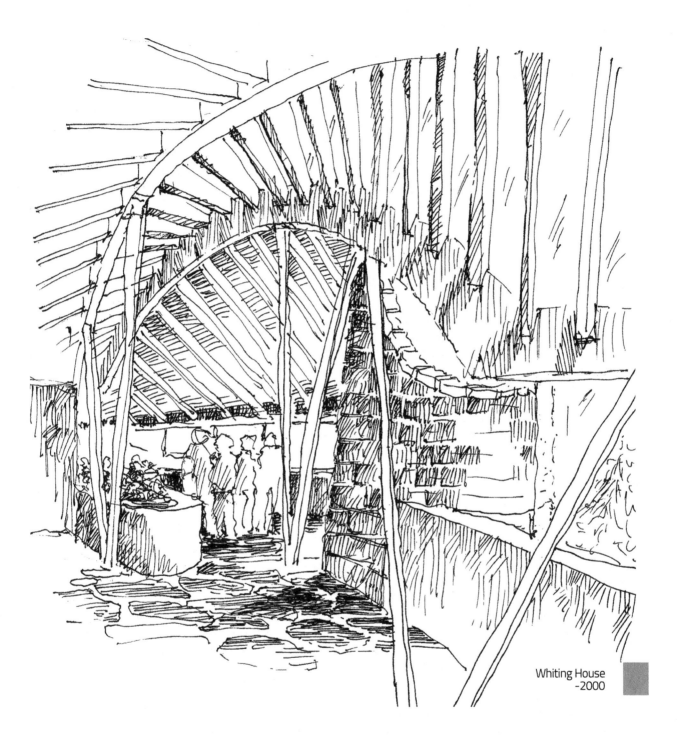

Whiting House
-2000

helped architects in Idaho plan a regional conference in Sun Valley. After one of the meetings, I spent a little free time visiting the Idaho State Capitol building. I sat in an available chair in the rotunda and proceeded to sketch the stately Greek Revival Corinthian columns and magnificent sweeping curve of the rotunda balcony. The arch-roofed Whiting house in Sun Valley, designed by Bart Prince, echoes the surrounding landscape and is a world apart in design from the classical forms of the state house.

ILLINOIS

Everywhere I walked while visiting Chicago's city center, I found a "picture perfect" scene to record.

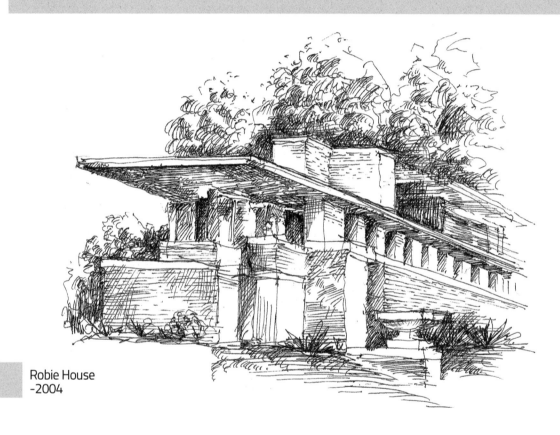

Robie House
-2004

Frank Lloyd Wright's Robie House, built in 1909, is an icon of his early work. Both this sketch and those of downtown Chicago depicting the Wrigley Building and Tribune Tower are memorable because my brother and I stood side-by-side drawing these scenes. His focus was different from mine, but I can tell we are drawing from the same location. The "Chicago Towers" sketch was done from a hotel window. Note the contrast between the turn of the century truncated masonry buildings in the foreground and the towering glass skyscrapers in the background. Skyscrapers were first built in Chicago. The structures were made possible after a Chicagoan named Elisha Otis invented a safety brake for elevators in 1853.

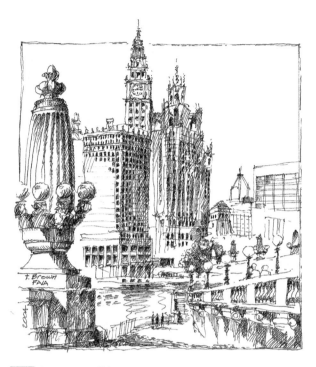

Downtown Chicago
-2004

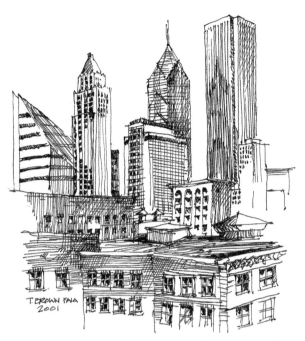

Chicago Towers
-2001

Chicago Stock Exchange
-2001

Lobby of the Palmer House
-2001

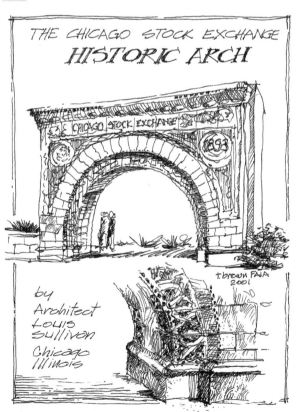

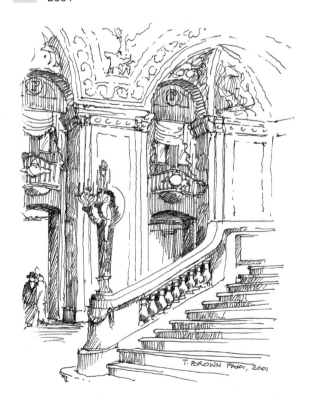

KENTUCKY

was invited to the home of the Louisville Slugger oak baseball bats in Kentucky to provide a Disaster Assistance training seminar to members of the Louisville American Institute of Architects. It rained constantly while I was there, forcing me to sketch a quick, very loose street scene from my hotel window early in the morning before taking a cab to the airport.

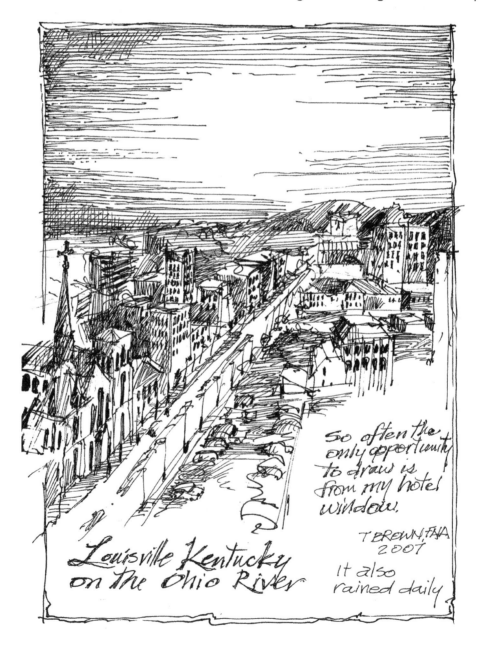

So often the only opportunity to draw is from my hotel window.

T. BROWN, FAIA
2007

It also rained daily

Louisville Kentucky on the Ohio River

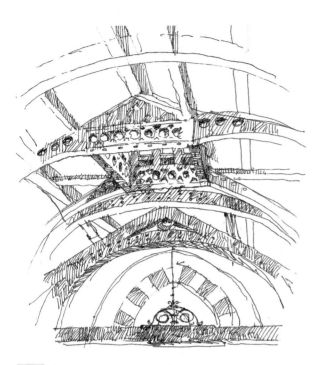

∧ Ceiling Beam Old South Church in Boston

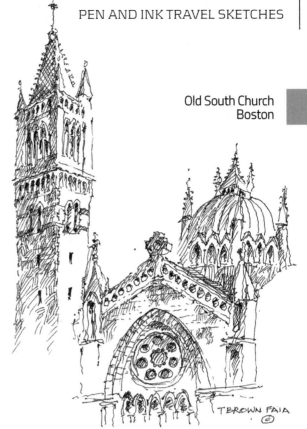

Old South Church
Boston

MASSACHUSETTS

The tall spires of Boston's churches are especially good drawing subjects. The brick Park Street Church, with its white wood steeple, is a fantastic example of what a proper protestant church looked like anywhere in America during the early years of our Republic. In contrast, the stone Romanesque Old South Church by English architect and critic John Ruskin is a colorful model of Northern Italian Gothic architecture that also illustrates the opulent taste of the Industrial Revolution. In this church in 1773, Samuel Adams gave the signal to begin the Boston Tea Party.

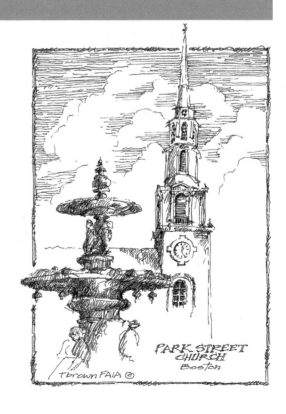

Michigan's two Grand Haven lighthouses fascinated me, so I sat on the beach to sketch them. The wind off the lake was fierce, so I packed up and walked to the lighthouse at the end of the pier. As I circled back, I was impressed with the size and conical shape of the 1905 structure. I decided to sketch this lighthouse over the scene I had started to draw from the coast. To complete the drawing, I framed the distant scene to appear like a postcard with the lighthouse superimposed over it.

Grand Haven Lighthouse -2013

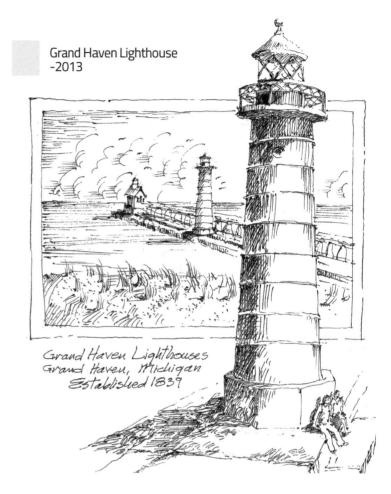

Grand Haven Lighthouses
Grand Haven, Michigan
Established 1839

MICHIGAN

Grand Rapids Bridge

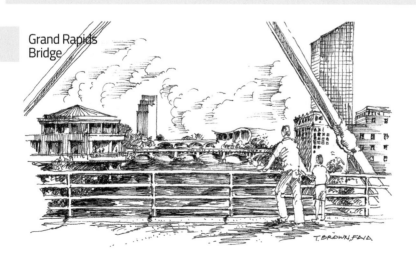

T.BROWN,FWA

Grand Rapids is the home of President Gerald Ford. I visited his unassuming Presidential Museum along the edge of Grand River, but found the river view of the city from the old bridge more interesting to sketch.

MONTANA

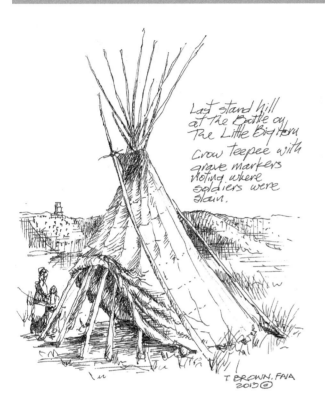

Last stand hill at The Battle on The Little Big Horn Crow teepee with grave markers noting where soldiers were slain.

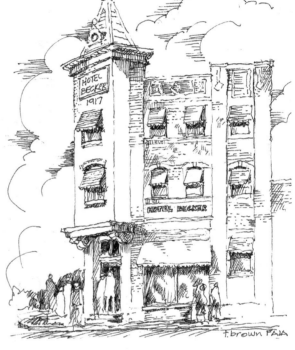

Last Stand Hill Teepee
- 2013

Becker Hotel
Hardin

On a hot day in 1876, on a hillside in south central Montana, General George Armstrong Custer and all his men were annihilated. It was the 100th anniversary of the United States. History notes that Custer divided his force and attacked a Sioux and Cheyenne tipi village along the Little Big Horn River, 12 miles from where I grew up. Custer's 7th Cavalry was stopped by some 1,000 battle hardened warriors, and he and his men were forced to flee up Medicine Tail Coulee to high ground in the last large scale Indian battle in the West.

The Becker Hotel, currently a bed and breakfast, was built in 1917 across the street from the train station of my home town of Hardin, Montana. I sketched the hotel during one of my high school reunions.

NEVADA

My wife and I were married in exciting Las Vegas, however, the rural, natural areas of Nevada, like Lake Tahoe, hold a stronger attraction for us.

I find it interesting how Las Vegas developers and architects build grand hotels and casinos singularly around historic themes. The Treasure Island Casino featured nightly staged pirate battles in "Buccaneer Bay" in front of the casino where pirates are also caught sacking a Caribbean village. Farther down the Strip, the Venetian Casino Hotel replicates historic buildings from Venice, Italy, at the entry and on the interior. Men in striped shirts and flat brimmed hats row guests in gondolas along a watery canal with clouds painted on the ceiling of the casino's interior.

Treasure Island Casino

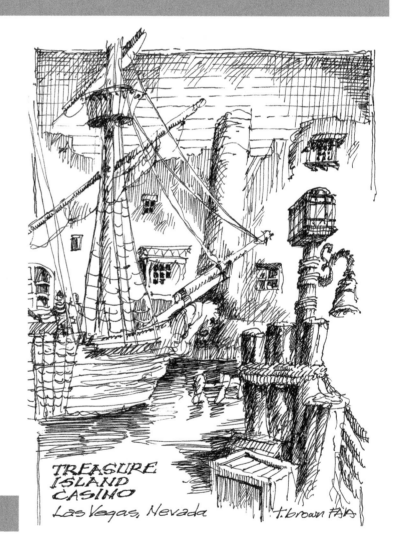

TREASURE ISLAND CASINO
Las Vegas, Nevada
t.brown FAIA

Stunningly beautiful, Lake Tahoe is a clear blue, 1,645 ft. deep lake and is the second largest in the country. Surrounded by the pine covered mountains, it is a natural wonder on the border of Nevada and California, overlooked all too aften by the draw of glitzy Las Vegas to the south.

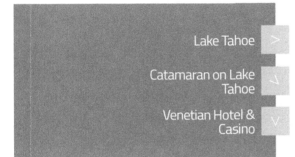

Lake Tahoe >

Catamaran on Lake Tahoe ∨

Venetian Hotel & Casino ∨

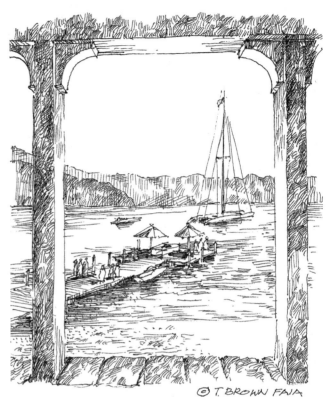

© T. BROWN FAIA

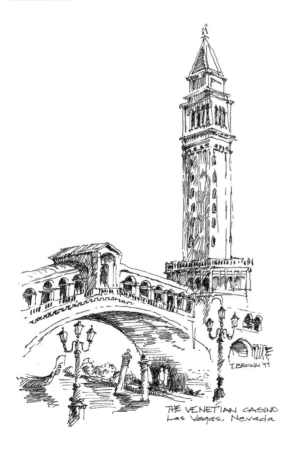

THE VENETIAN CASINO
Las Vegas, Nevada

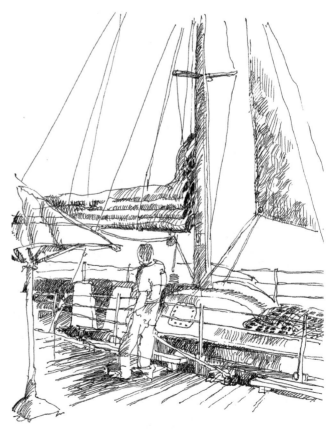

NEW JERSEY

Nassau Hall
Tower

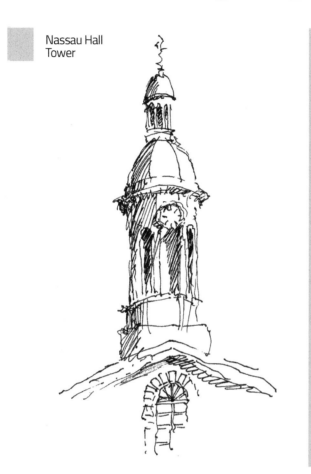

On a trip to Newark, I had absolutely no time to tour the city because wintery darkness closed in early around my airport hotel. Thus I sketched the parking lot from my room on the 12th floor. The lion's head wood carving detail on this table in Princeton University's Nassau Hall is magnificent. All of Princeton University is awash with historic architecture, Palmer Square, across the street from the campus, was created in the Colonial Revival Style in 1939 by Edgar Palmer, heir to the New Jersey zinc fortune. While at Princeton, the AIA Board of Directors was invited to a reception at the home of AIA Gold Medal recipient, Michael Graves, FAIA. I asked Mr. Graves to do a drawing of one of his iconic buildings in my sketchbook which he graciously provided. I added his drawing to my collection of drawings by famous architects.

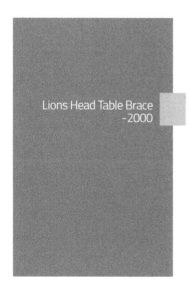

Lions Head Table Brace
-2000

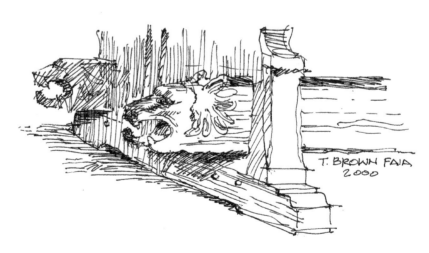

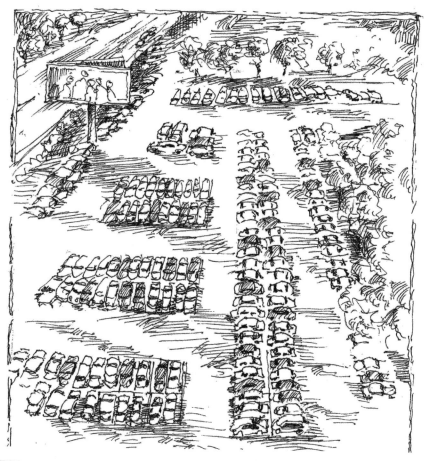

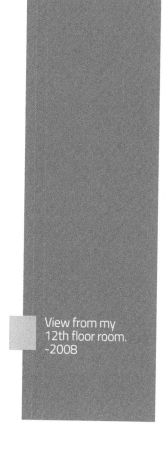

View from my
12th floor room.
-2008

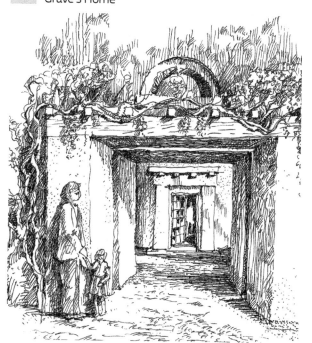

Gateway to Michael
Grave's Home

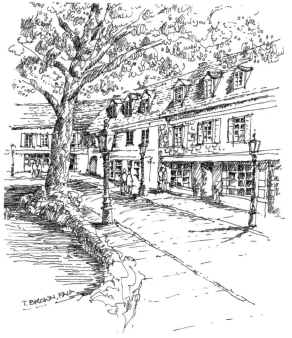

Palmer Square
-2000

NEW MEXICO

"

This drawing celebrates the first buildings on each of the first three university campuses in New Mexico. The building named "The University" has been drastically remodeled to emulate a flat roofed pueblo building.

New Mexico Architecture Magazine

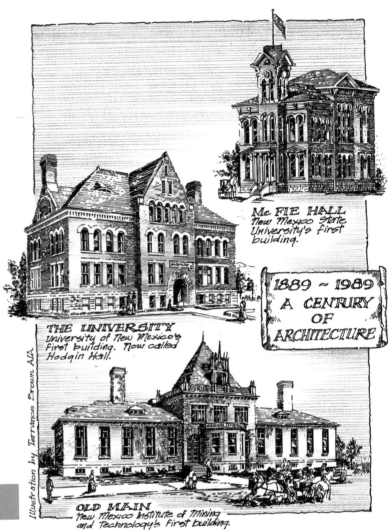

Mc FIE HALL
New Mexico State University's first building.

1889 ~ 1989
A CENTURY
OF
ARCHITECTURE

THE UNIVERSITY
University of New Mexico's first building. Now called Hodgin Hall.

Illustration by Terrance Brown AIA

OLD MAIN
New Mexico Institute of Mining and Technology's first building.

The Pueblo Revival style of architecture, seen throughout most of New Mexico, emulates the adobe and mud plastered stone walls of the ancient Native American pueblos. Adobe walls, small windows and flat roofs with parapets protect the home from the elements and blend with the landscape. Today this type of building system is construction with wood framing and a stucco finish system. Tan or brown are popular color choices.

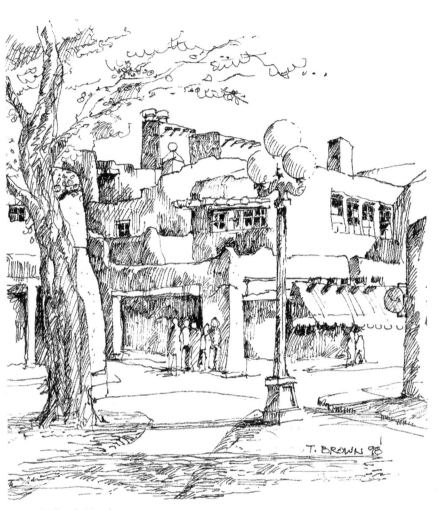

> Earth color stucco is a prolific wall surfacing material seen across New Mexico. The color emulates original mud plaster on early adobe structures.

La Fonda Hotel
Santa Fe
-1989

House
Sandia Foothills
-1989

Rio Grande House
Albuquerque
-1989

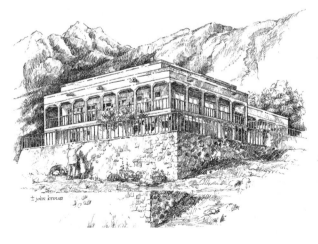

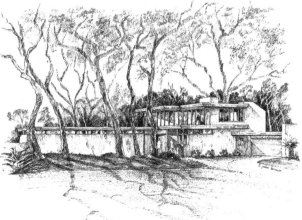

"

Many historic communities in New Mexico, regardless of size, have a church or chapel, very often located on one side of a plaza at the center of town.

Laguna Church

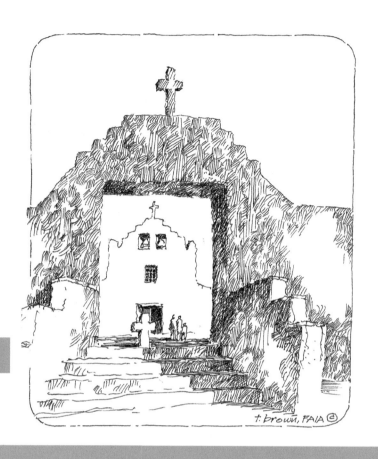

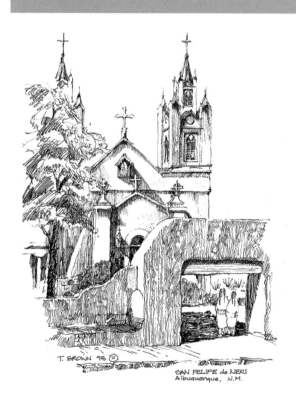

SAN FELIPE de NERI
Albuquerque, N.M.

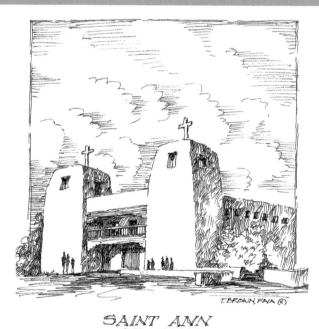

SAINT ANN
MISSION
ACOMITA,   NEW MEXICO
ACOMA PUEBLO

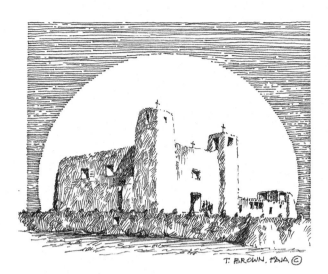

SAN ESTEVAN del REY
~
ESTABLISHED 1629

ACOMA PUEBLO, NEW MEXICO

ACOMA PUEBLO WAS FOUNDED
IN THE LATE 1200'S ON TOP OF
A 350 FOOT HIGH MESA

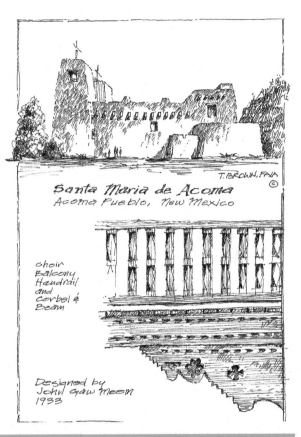

T. BROWN, FAIA ©

Santa Maria de Acoma
Acoma Pueblo, New Mexico

choir
Balcony
Handrail
and
corbel &
Beam

Designed by
John Gaw Meem
1933

After conquering Mexico, the Spaniards entered the New Mexico Territory in 1540. Soon after they began to build churches in the pueblos with forced labor. The enormous San Estevan del Rey Church at Acoma Pueblo is an example of pueblo style construction. Heavy stone and adobe walls, wood logs bearing the roof and mud plastering were provided with great effort. Many more churches in New Mexico were built by local families.

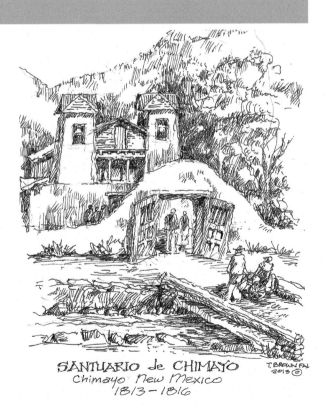

SANTUARIO de CHIMAYO
Chimayo New Mexico
1813 – 1816

T BROWN FAI
2013 ©

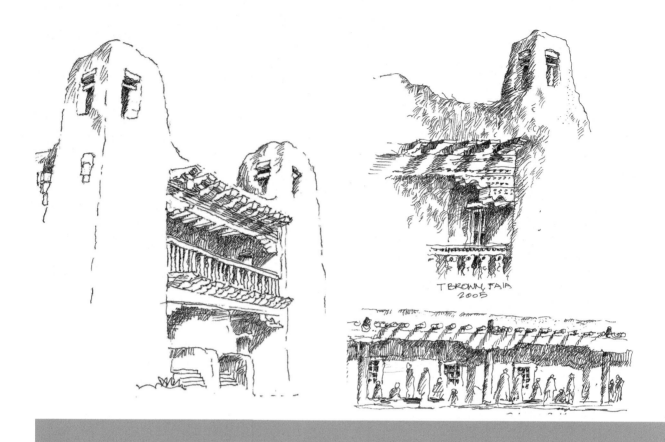

T BROWN, FAIA
2005

The details in New Mexican houses and public buildings emulate the popular Pueblo Revival Style of architecture. Simple wood columns are crowned by decorative corbels. The kiva style corner fireplace, found in many Native American Pueblo homes, is often seen in modern homes as well. Many churches in New Mexico were built by families living in the small towns. El Santuario de Chimayo (on the previous page), a small church in northern New Mexico, was built in 1816 and is believed to provide strength to people in search of spiritual and physical healing.

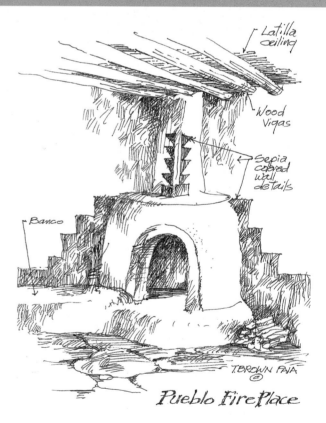

Latilla ceiling

Wood Vigas

Sepia colored wall details

Banco

T.BROWN FAIA

Pueblo FirePlace

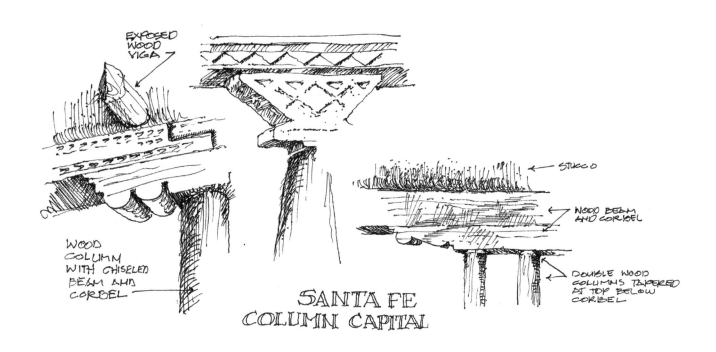

EXPOSED WOOD VIGA

WOOD COLUMN WITH CHISELED BEAM AND CORBEL

STUCCO

WOOD BEAM AND CORBEL

DOUBLE WOOD COLUMNS TAPERED AT TOP BELOW CORBEL

SANTA FE
COLUMN CAPITAL

Our Lady of
Sorrows Church

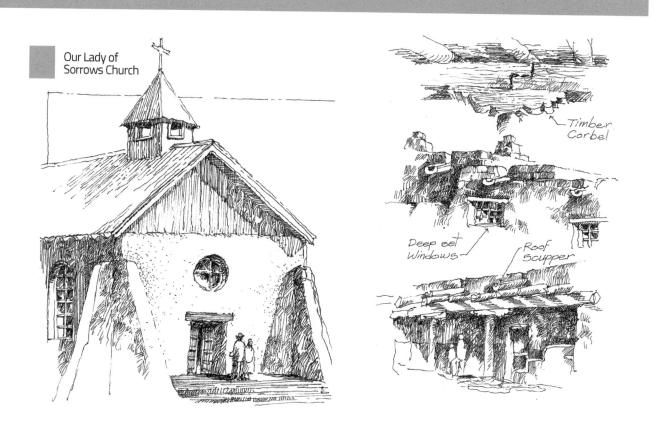

Timber Corbel

Deep set Windows

Roof Scupper

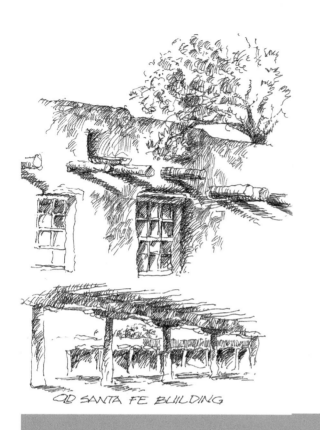

OLD SANTA FE BUILDING

The drawing on the right titled Los Poblanos Ranch was produced during one of my Field Sketching Academy classes. I ask all students to draw the same scene and compare drawings. In mine, arching tree branches help frame the barn's silo.

New Mexico architecture and building details are as varied as they are visually intriguing. Native American cultures abound throughout the state, and pueblo design elements are often replicated in new buildings.

The ruins of a large Catholic Church is sited awkwardly beside this kiva at Pecos National Monument. The below ground, single room kiva is still used for religious training and ritual dances by the men and boys of the pueblo.

Kimo Theater
Albuquerque, NM

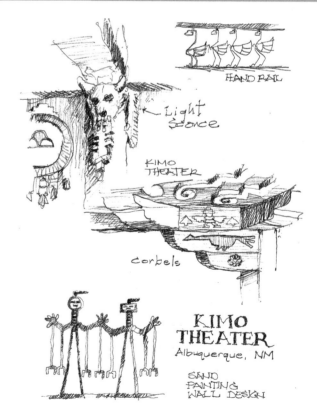

HAND RAIL

Light Sconce

KIMO THEATER

corbels

KIMO THEATER
Albuquerque, NM

SAND PAINTING WALL DESIGN

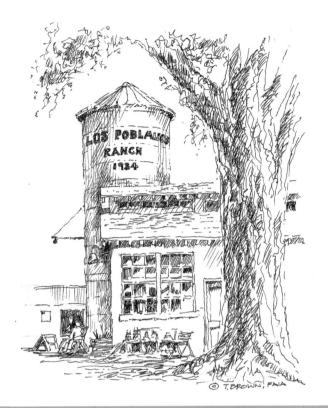

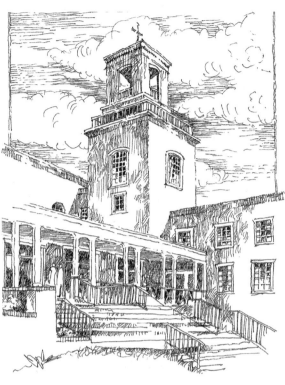

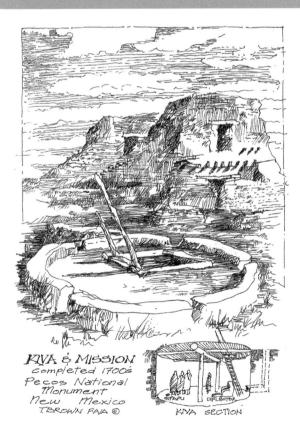

KIVA & MISSION
completed 1700s
Pecos National
Monument
New Mexico
T.BROWN FAIA ©

KIVA SECTION

Los Poblanos Farm

Immanual
Presbyterian Church

Kiva and Mission
Peco National Monument

For the past 30 years, along with New Mexico Military Institute alumni friends, I have attended annual trail rides on various cattle ranches across New Mexico. I sketch scenes from this ride and each year the drawings are auctioned off. The proceeds from the sale support a Trail Ride Scholarship I created to help young graduates from New Mexico Military Institute attend the ride.

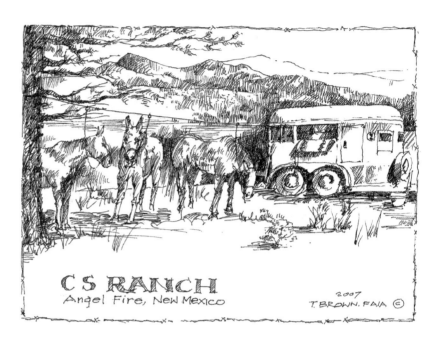

CS RANCH
Angel Fire, New Mexico
2007
T. BROWN. FAIA ©

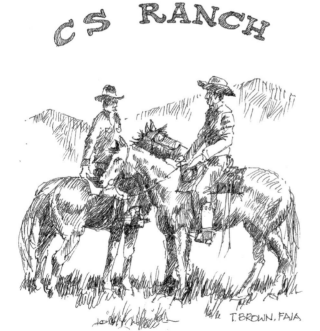

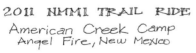

2011 NMMI TRAIL RIDE
American Creek Camp
Angel Fire, New Mexico

T. BROWN, FAIA

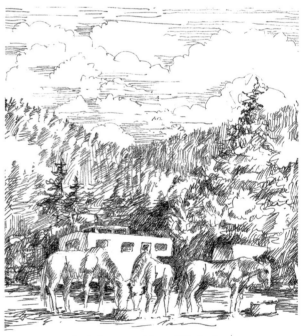

~ After the Ride ~
on the CS RANCH

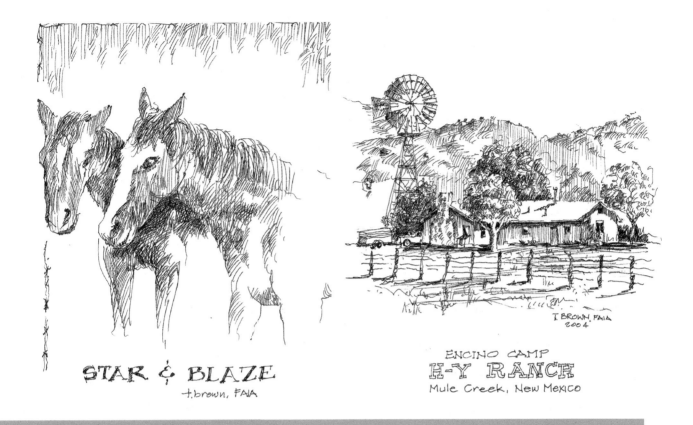

STAR & BLAZE
t.brown, FAIA

ENCINO CAMP
H-Y RANCH
Mule Creek, New Mexico

T. BROWN, FAIA
2004

"

Horses often stand still, making them easy and approachable subjects.

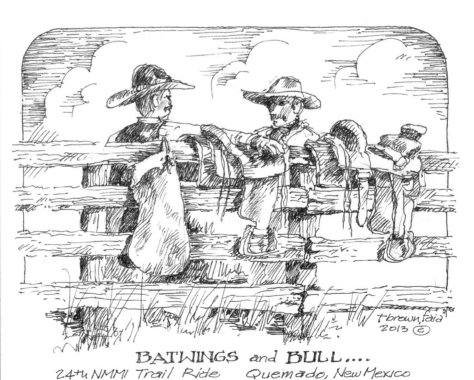

t.brown, faia
2013 ©

BATWINGS and BULL....
24th NMMI Trail Ride   Quemado, New Mexico

NEW YORK

The terrorist attack on The World Trade Center will always be with me, but the 911 Memorial on the same site provides hope and honors the lives of those who died that day.

Guggenheim Museum by
Frank Lloyd Wright

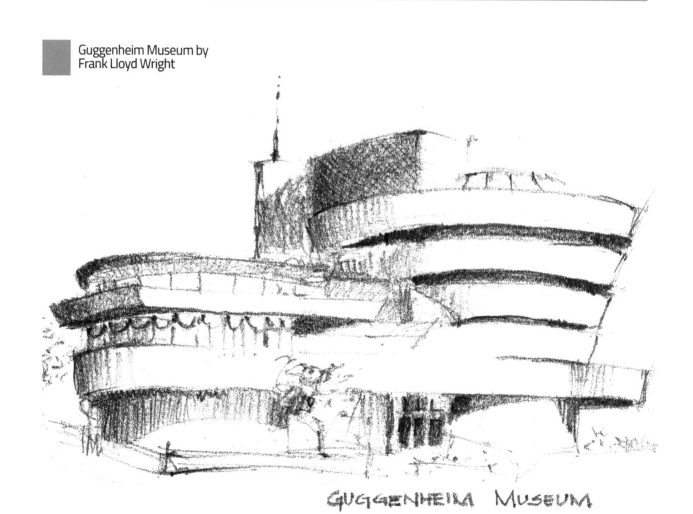

GUGGENHEIM MUSEUM

> It was strange to observe that giant pit and remember that tragic day in 2001.

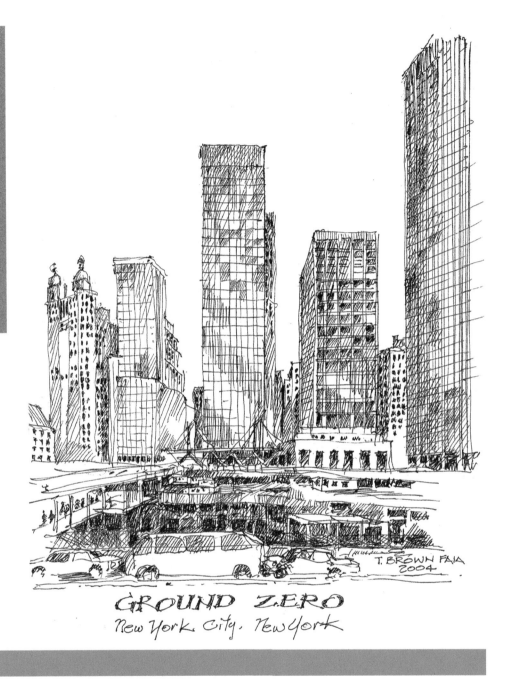

GROUND ZERO
New York City, New York

T. BROWN FAIA
2004

first visited New York City with my brother on the way to Europe to tour the buildings we studied in architecture history classes. The pencil drawing of the Guggenheim Museum by Frank Lloyd Wright was made during that trip. Many years later, I checked into a hotel beside the gaping hole in the ground at Ground Zero where the World Trade Center once stood. It was strange to observe that giant pit and remember that tragic September day in 2001 when terrorists toppled the two skyscrapers by flying passenger planes into them.

OKLAHOMA

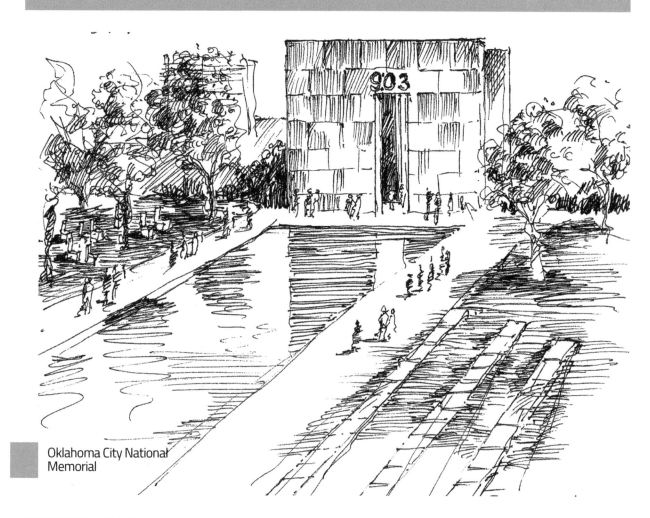

Oklahoma City National Memorial

The Oklahoma city National Memorial is a monument to hope. It records the time, 9:03 AM, when a truck bomb blasted through the Murrah Federal Building, killing 168 people including 19 children. The Field of Chairs is a poignant reminder of each life lost; instead of names on a wall, translucent chairs, one for each person, rest on the site of the bombed Federal Building. The rectangular reflecting pool is sited where the street once passed in front of the building.

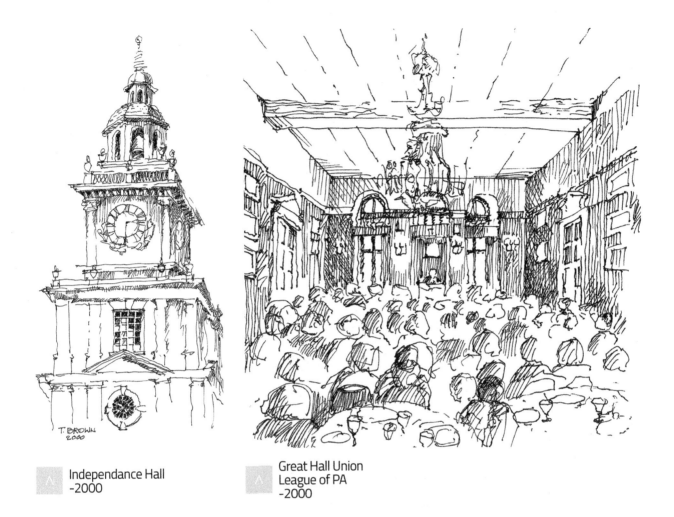

Λ Independance Hall
-2000

Λ Great Hall Union
League of PA
-2000

PENNSYLVANIA

This state has witnessed much of the history of our nation's founding. Sketching the Great Hall of the Union League fully populated adds a human touch and scale to this relatively simple room.

One can easily imagine, while standing in this room, when friends of Abraham Lincoln gathered together in the space to support his policies. I could not leave Philadelphia without sketching the white painted tower of Independence Hall, which was completed in 1753. The Hall is known primarily as the location where both the United States Constitution and Declaration of Independence were debated and adopted.

SOUTH DAKOTA

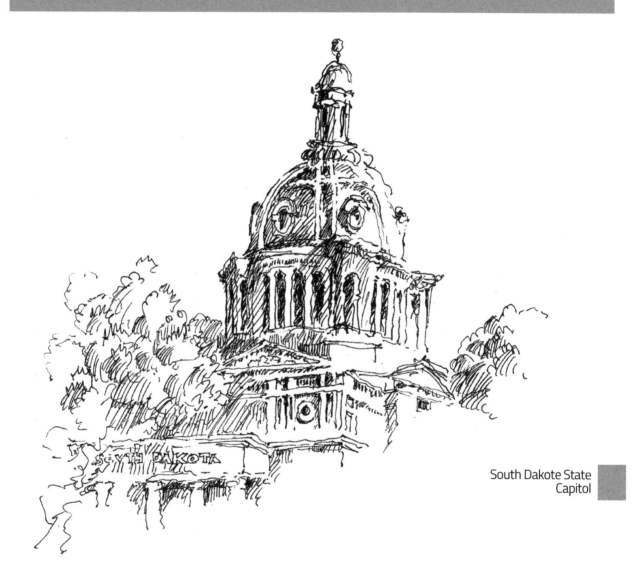

South Dakote State
Capitol

I was amazed by the grandeur of the South Dakota State Capitol building, which is modeled after Montana's State Capitol. South Dakota is the 5th least populous and 5th least densely populated of the US. It was granted statehood in 1889, along with North Dakota, and is named after the Lakota and Dakota Sioux American Indian tribes. Over the years I designed various South Dakota hospitals, medical clinics and over 100 staff quarters for the Indian Health Service as well as homes for the Yankton, Santee, Rosebud, Cheyenne River and Pine Ridge Sioux tribes.

Tennessee State Capitol
-2000

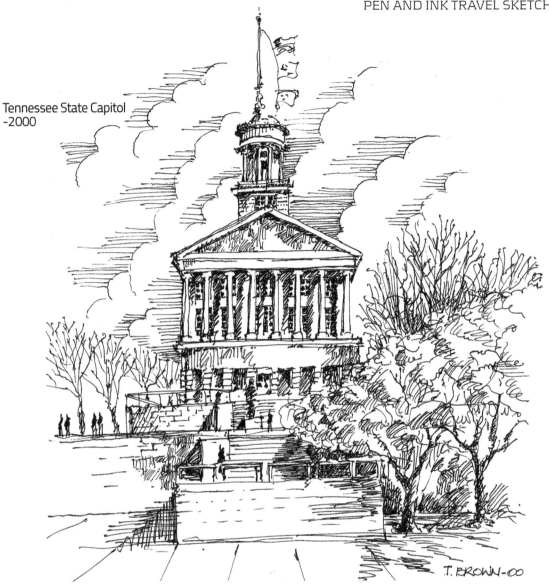

T. BROWN-00

TENNESSEE

The Tennesse state capitol is an impressive Greek revival style building form and a genuine contrast to many domed capitol buildings.

According to *A Global History of Architecture* by Francis Ching, "the American's saw their nation as the land of opportunity, where they could return to classical values without the

encumbrance of custom." This style of building is not an isolated example, but was popular and prevalent across the US and Canada.

TEXAS

One morning while I was in Fort Worth sketching the Tarrant County Courthouse, I heard on television that a tornado had just killed 40 people. I felt compelled to draw a tornado ripping across the scene.

I have a strong connection to Texas—I earned my Bachelor of Architecture Degree from Texas Tech University and completed my architectural internship in El Paso, where I also received my license to practice architecture.

Kimball Art Museum
-1999

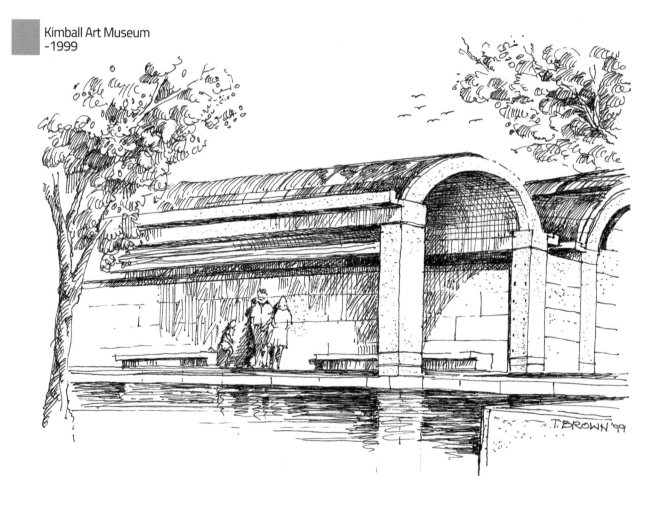

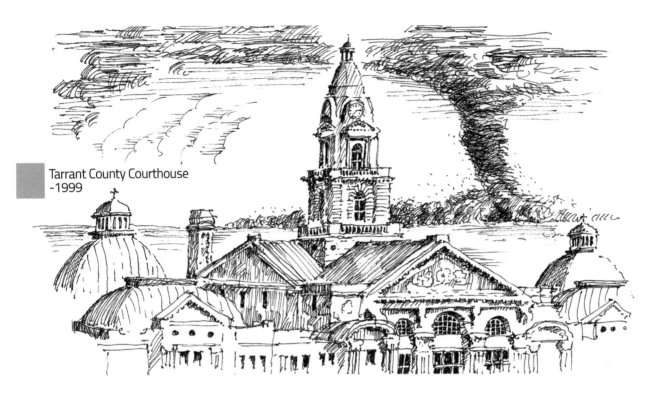

Tarrant County Courthouse
-1999

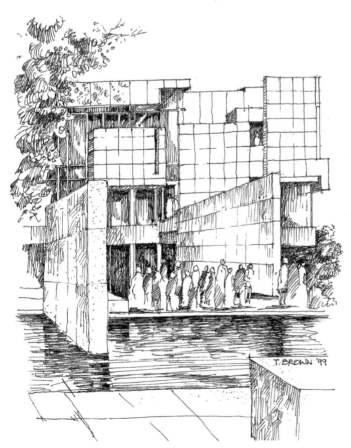

"

The Rachofsky House by AIA Gold Medal recipient Richard Meier, FAIA, is unique in its linear design, which made it more difficult to draw freehand.

Rachofsky House
-1999

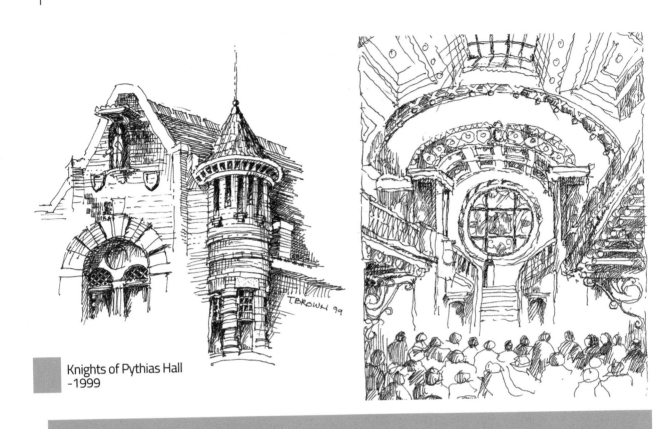

Knights of Pythias Hall
-1999

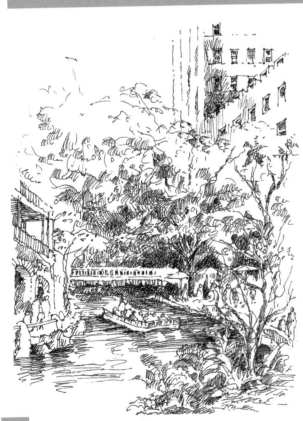

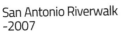
San Antonio Riverwalk
-2007

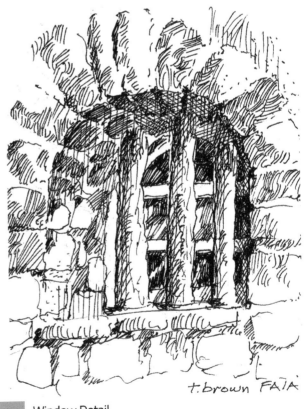
Window Detail
Long Barrack - The Alamo

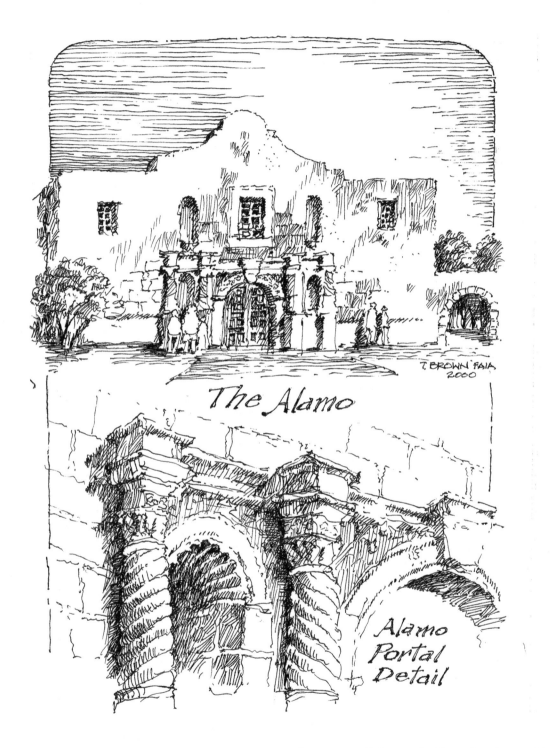

The Alamo

Alamo
Portal
Detail

The battle of the Alamo, where Davy Crocket, William Travis, Jim Bowie and many other brave men died defending Texas from Santa Anna's Mexican army, became a rallying cry for Texas freedom and is now a shrine to these defenders. I found myself sketching fast and furiously, full of emotion, while capturing the details of this historic building and site.

UTAH

By drawing mundane, everyday elements and scenes you record the moment and wind up with memorable drawings in your portfolio.

During a layover at the Salt Lake City airport, I sketched this view of a Delta Airline's gate and loading area. The detail and texture of this drawing transforms a mundane scene and records a moment in time in a way a photograph cannot. The figures, scattered baggage carts, walkway, airplane tails and light poles add character and depth to an otherwise unassuming airport scene.

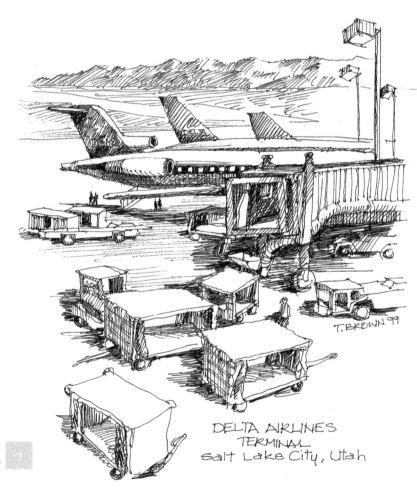

DELTA AIRLINES
TERMINAL
Salt Lake City, Utah

T.BROWN 99

Delta Airlines Terminal
-1999

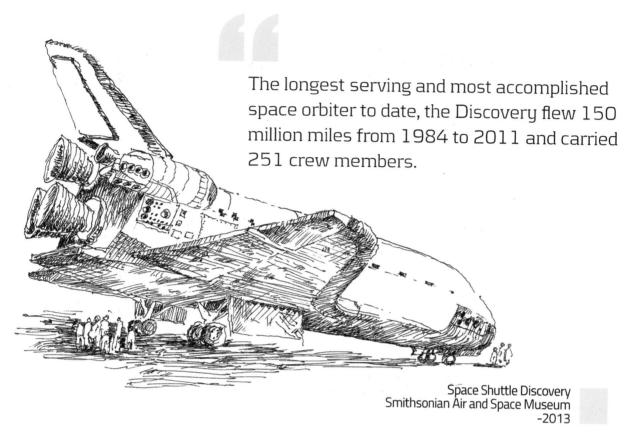

The longest serving and most accomplished space orbiter to date, the Discovery flew 150 million miles from 1984 to 2011 and carried 251 crew members.

Space Shuttle Discovery
Smithsonian Air and Space Museum
-2013

VIRGINIAS

As a 1st Assistance Scoutmaster, I lead 23 boys from New Mexico and Colorado to the Boy Scout National Jamboree at Summit Bechtel Reserve, the BSA's new high adventure camp in West Virginia's forested mountains. Over 36,500 boys and leaders from 18 countries attended. It was extremely hot, rainy and muddy, but we had new waterproof dome tents and cots, lots to eat and plenty of fun. Drawing was a terrific way to document the experience.

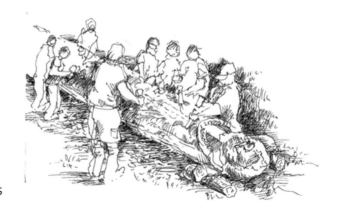

Carving the National Eagle Scout Pole
-2013 National BSA Jamboree

Mount Vernon
-2003

Monticello
-2013

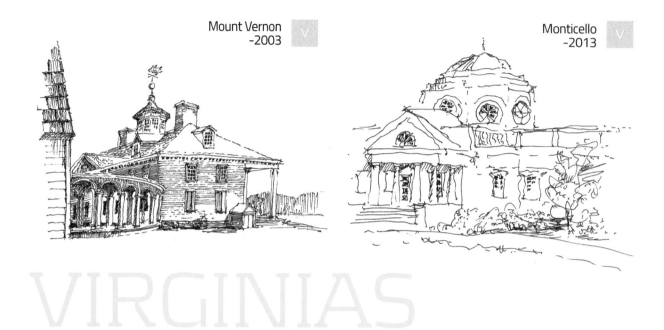

VIRGINIAS

Mount Vernon was the home of our first president, George Washington, and is an American architectural treasure. In winter I walked the snow covered side yard to sketch one façade of the house and a covered walkway leading to an outbuilding. After starting the drawing, I decided to include detail of the home's iconic front elevation as well. I sketched Monticello, Thomas Jefferson's home, in under five minutes to capture just the essence of this stately house. The Manassas National Battlefield sits in the peaceful Virginia countryside, yet it once witnessed two major clashes between the Union and Confederate Armies during the Civil War. General Thomas J. Jackson, one of the most gifted tactical commanders of the Civil War, acquired his nickname "Stonewall" during the first battle on this site.

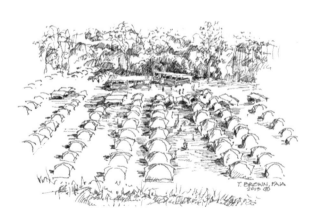

BSA National Jamboree
-2013

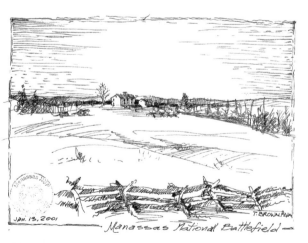

Manassas National Battlefield
-2001

WASHINGTON

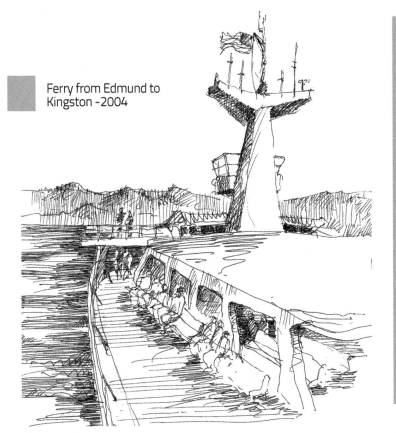

Ferry from Edmund to
Kingston -2004

Water is ubiquitous along the coastal areas of Washington, and views towards the water can create interesting drawings. Sketching the ferry crossing from Seattle to the Olympic Peninsula helped me pass the time and connected me more to the experience of that journey.

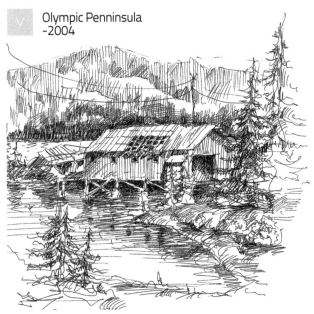

Olympic Penninsula
-2004

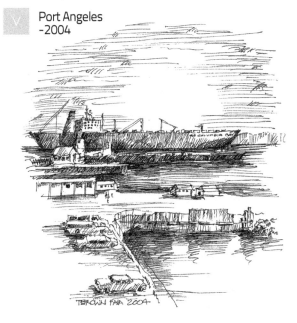

Port Angeles
-2004

WASHINGTON DC

The buildings of the US capital may feel too imposing and intricate to draw. Try focusing on a specific element. You can expand your drawing from there or let the detail serve as representation of your experience.

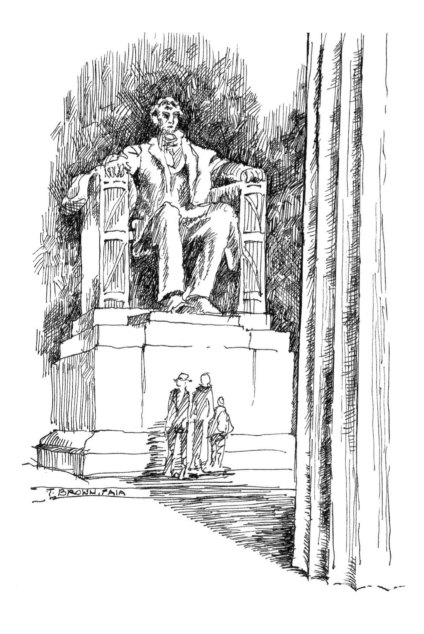

Washington, DC, the US capital, is a compact city on the Potomac River, bordering the states of Maryland and Virginia. It is defined by imposing neoclassical monuments and buildings—including the iconic ones that house the federal government's three branches: the Capitol, White House and Supreme Court. Yet the city's architecture reflects the eras of our collective history—from the country's founding to icons of contemporary experience.

Lincoln Memorial
-2001

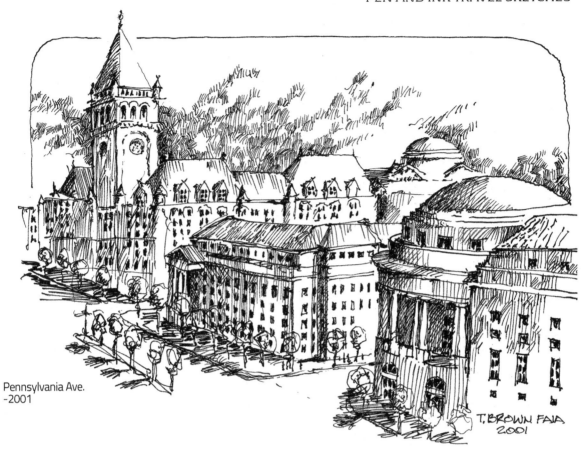

Pennsylvania Ave.
-2001

AIA Headquarters
-2003

The Octagon House
-1999

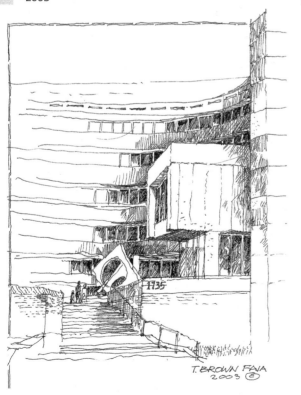

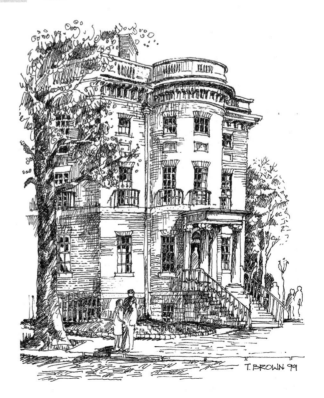

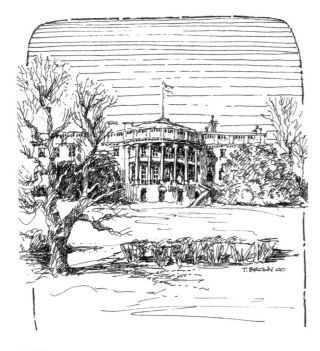

∧ The White House
   -2000

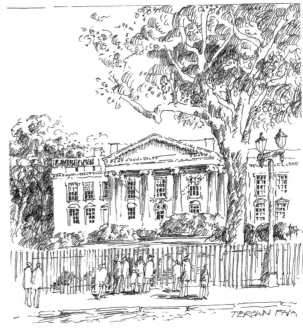

∧ The White House

E very visit to our nation's capital city offers an opportunity to sketch historic buildings. Once, while drawing the White House during a bone chilling freeze, I had to keep stuffing my drawing hand into my coat to warm my fingers. Because of the intense winter cold, this Treasury Building sketch was drawn looking out my hotel window. The US Capitol building so dominates Capitol Hill, that I found myself sketching its dome several times over the years.

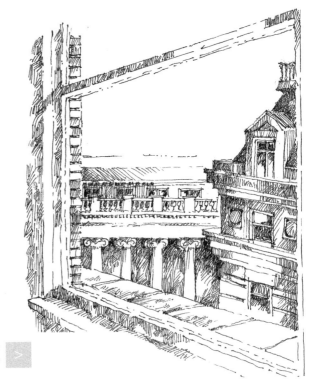

The US Treasury >
from my hotel window

Old Stone House (1766)
-1999

The Castle
The Smithsonian Institute
-2001

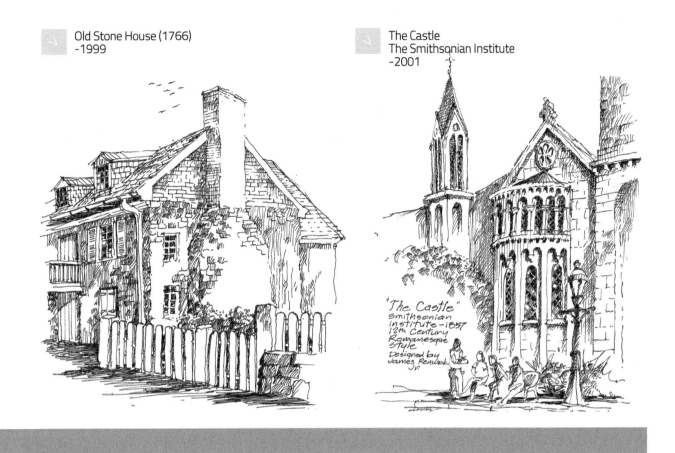

US Capitol
-2001

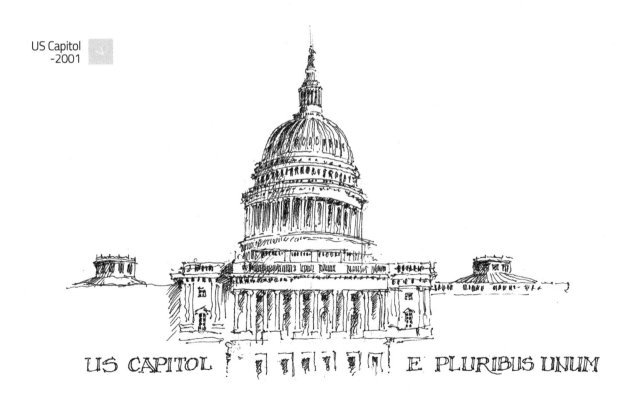

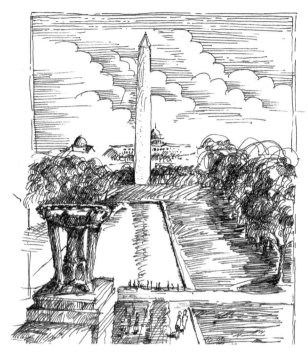

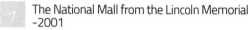 The National Mall from the Lincoln Memorial
-2001

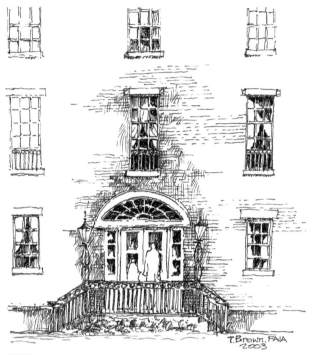

Decatur House (1818)
-2003

The Chesapeake and Ohio Canal in Georgetown are part of a canal system that extends from Georgetown, DC, to Cumberland, Maryland. It took 22 years to construct and operated for nearly 100 years. The canal provided transportation for people and goods along the Potomac River. Historians estimate it took 35,000 immigrant laborers from Ireland and Western Europe to dig the canal and build the buildings and locks. Nearly as soon as the entire canal system was complete, the railroad made it obsolete.

Chesapeake & Ohio Canal
-1999

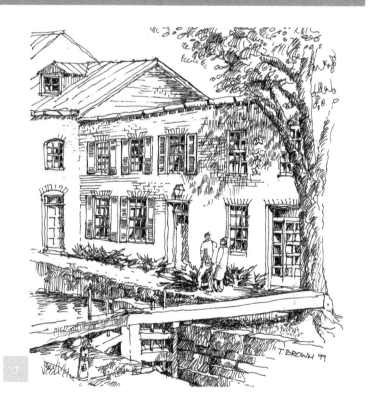

WISCONSIN

Romeo & Juliet Windmill
by Frank Lloyd Wright

This sixty foot tall windmill and water tower designed by Frank Lloyd Wright in 1897 evokes strong memories from my visit to Wright's large summer home in Spring Green. The unique tower was constructed of interlocking diamond and octagonal wooden forms and, contrary to some accounts, has stood for nearly 100 years.

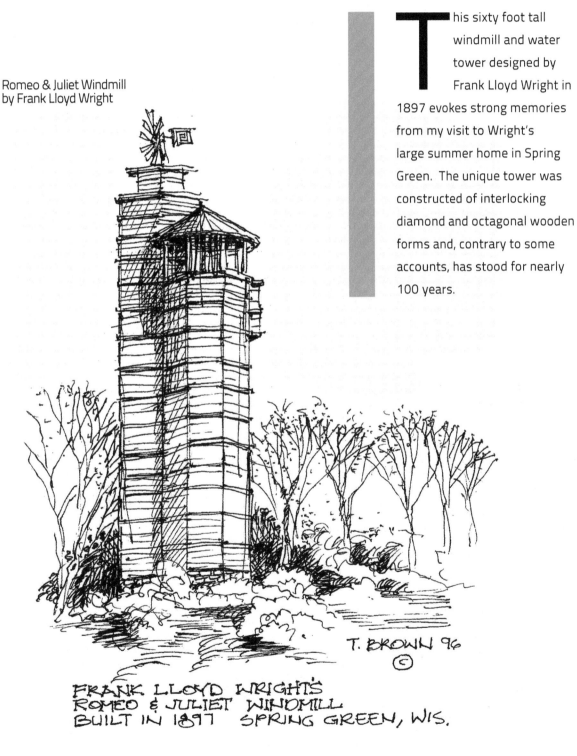

T. BROWN 96
ⓒ

FRANK LLOYD WRIGHT'S
ROMEO & JULIET WINDMILL
BUILT IN 1897 SPRING GREEN, WIS.

WYOMING

We were anxious to check into the beautiful log hotel at Yellowstone National Park after the airplanes attacked the World Trade Center towers and were disappointed our rooms had no TVs or radios to follow the news.

Old Faithful Inn
Details
-1999

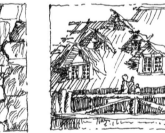
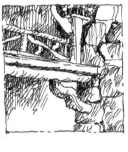
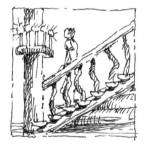
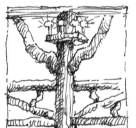
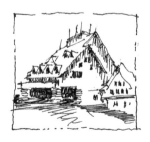
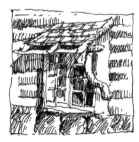

The Old Faithful Inn was constructed in Yellowstone National Park during the winter of 1903-1904. When this handsome example of rustic resort architecture (also known as National Park Rustic) first opened, it boasted electric lights and steam heat—new technologies at the time. The lodge is the largest log hotel in the world. A 2007 survey of the 150 favorite buildings in the world ranked this building 36th.

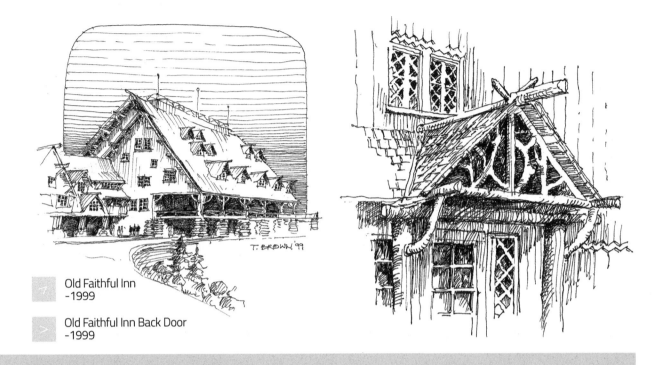

Old Faithful Inn
-1999

Old Faithful Inn Back Door
-1999

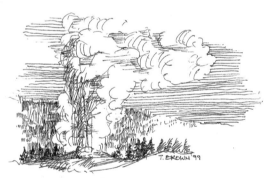

Old Faithful Lower Falls
-1999

Old Faithful Inn
Interior
-1999

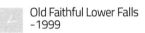

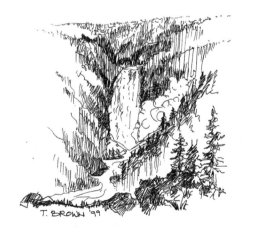

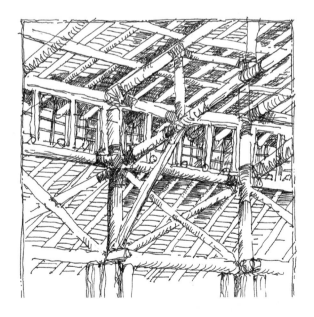

PEOPLE

While sitting through American Institute of Architects (AIA) meetings, I sketched the people and faces of attendees. Faces and the human form are particularly challenging to draw but well worth the effort. I enjoy looking back at these drawings and picking out the individuals I know. Understanding the anatomy of the human head and basic human proportions helps a great deal in these types of drawings: the eyes are about half way between the top of the head and the chin. The mouth is about half way from the bottom of the nose to the chin. The top of the ears are about level with the eyes. If you understand these proportions, the balance of facial details fall into place.

AIA International Presidents Forum >

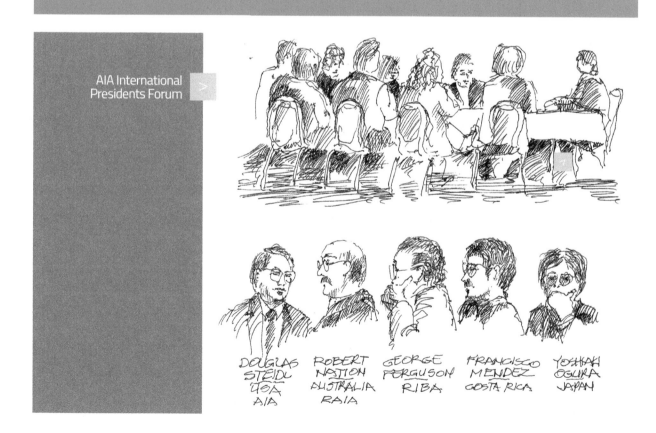

DOUGLAS STEIDL TSA AIA   ROBERT NATION AUSTRALIA RAIA   GEORGE FERGUSON RIBA   FRANCISCO MENDEZ COSTA RICA   YOSHIAKI OGURA JAPAN

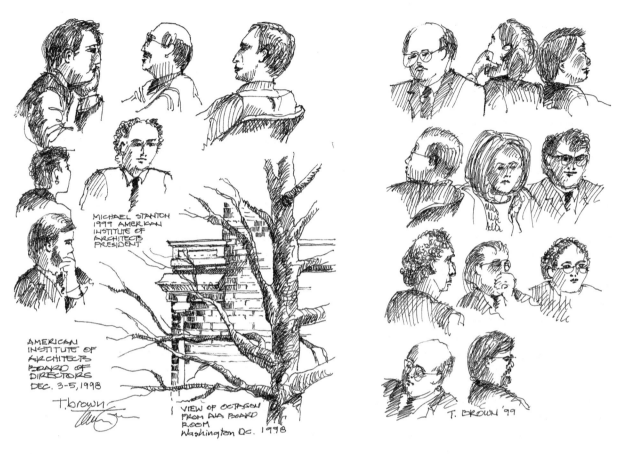

MICHAEL STANTON
1999 AMERICAN
INSTITUTE OF
ARCHITECTS
PRESIDENT

AMERICAN
INSTITUTE OF
ARCHITECTS
BOARD OF
DIRECTORS
DEC. 3-5, 1998

T. brown

VIEW OF OCTAGON
FROM AIA BOARD
ROOM
Washington DC. 1998

T. BROWN '99

 AIA Board of Directors
-1999

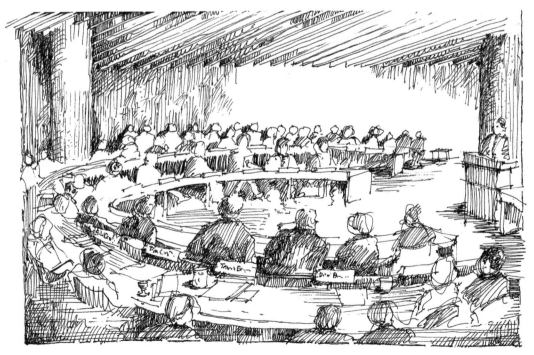

This detailed drawing of a Mayan man, with a hand-carved deer mask and ceremonial clothing, is one of my favorites. However, the quick drawings of people sketched during meetings and conferences bring back strong memories of friends and acquaintances. I always strove to rapidly capture unique characteristics of their faces or hair, their glasses, or facial hair. One day I was drawing a preacher during his sermon and looked over to observe my little daughters doing the same thing.

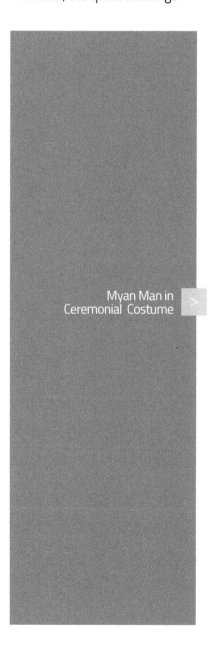

Myan Man in
Ceremonial Costume >

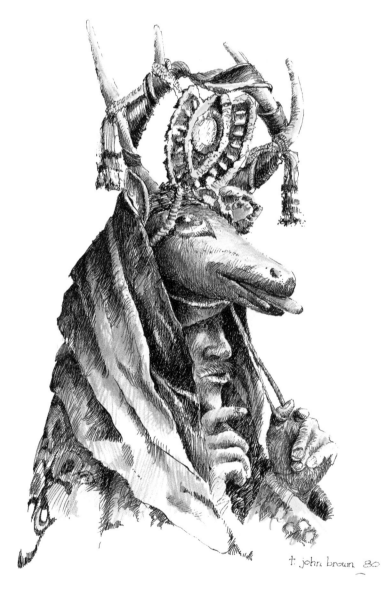

"
Drawing a group of people at a table is not that intimidating. Try drawing the back of their heads and shoulders before tackling faces.

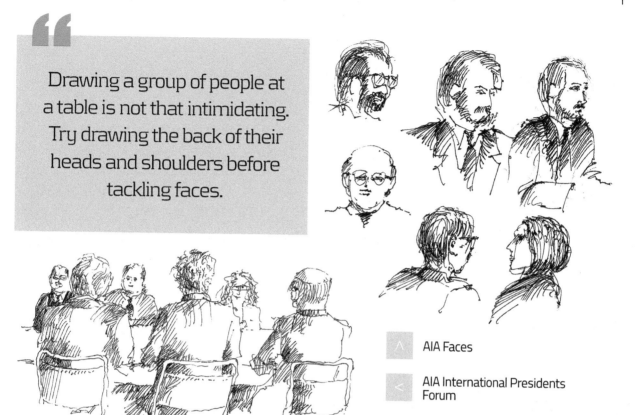

AIA Faces

AIA International Presidents Forum

 AIA Grassroots
–2007

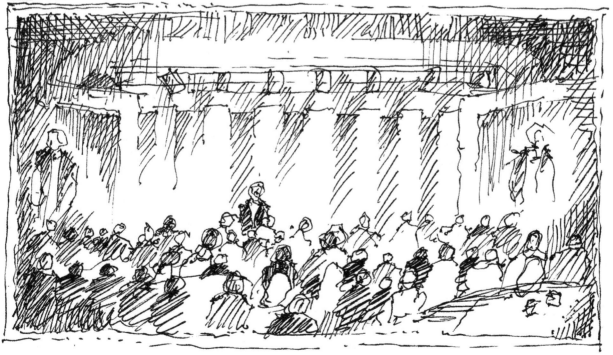

EDUCATION

Bachelor of Architecture, Texas Tech University (1964–1969)
Montana State University (1963–1964)

HONORS

American Institute of Architects Albuquerque New Mexico Lifetime Achievement Award (2016)
American Institute of Architects New Mexico Silver Medal for Lifetime Achievement (2013)
Edward C. Kemper Award (2016)
Whitney Young Jr. Award (2004)
Lancing B. Bloom Award, Historical Society of New Mexico (2003)
Richard Upjohn Fellow, Second Award (2001)
Texas Tech University Architecture Alumni Association Distinguished Alumnus (2001)
Western Mountain Region Silver Medal (highest award in 6 state region) (2000)
Fellow of the American Institute of Architects (2000)
Richard Upjohn Fellow, First Award (1999)

LEADERSHIP IN THE BOY SCOUTS OF AMERICA

Arrowman of the Year, Order of the Arrow (2016)
Distinguished Commissioner Award (2016)
Vigil Honor, Order of the Arrow, Yah-Tah-Hey-Si-Kess Lodge, (2016)
Silver Beaver Award (highest award in Great Southwest Council) (2015)
Doctorate of Commissioner Science Degree (2015)
Commissioner Award of Excellence in Unit Service Award (2014)
District Award of Merit (2012)
Eagle Scout (1962)

SERVICE TO THE PROFESSION

New Mexico Representative to the American Institute of Architects College of Fellows (2013 to present)
Chair, American Institute of Architects New Mexico Fellow Task Force (2011 to present)
American Institute of Architects Ambassador, Federation of Pan American Architect Associations, Panama, Costa Rica, Ecuador, Brazil, Mexico, Honduras, Guadalupe, Canada, Puerto Rico and Columbia, (2001 to 2007)
Chair, American Institute of Architects National Disaster Assistance Committee (2005–2007)
Member, American Institute of Architects National Disaster Assistance Committee (2004–2012)
North American Secretary, Federation of Pan American Architect Associations, Canada, USA, Mexico and Caribbean Islands (2004–2006)
Chair, International Honorary Fellows Jury, American Institute of Architects College of Fellows (2003)
Member, American Institute of Architects International Honorary Fellows Jury (2002)
Member, American Institute of Architects International Committee (2001–2006)
President, New Mexico Architectural Foundation (2001–2003)
Member, American Institute of Architects National Honor Awards Jury (2005)
Member, International Honorary Fellows Jury, College of Fellows (2001)
Vice President, The American Institute of Architects (2001)
Chancellor, American Institute of Architects National College of Drawers (2000)
Regional Director, American Institute of Architects Western Mountain Region (1996–1999)
Member, American Institute of Architects National Secretary Advisory Group (1996–1999)
President, American Institute of Architects New Mexico (1996)
President, American Institute of Architects Albuquerque, New Mexico (1991)

Note: Dates accurate as of the publication date of this book.

About the Author

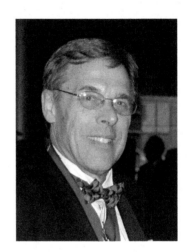

Terrance Brown developed his pen and ink drawing style as a student of architecture at Texas Tech University and began to carry a sketch book while traveling in Europe studying historic architecture. He enjoyed his drawings and their details much more than photographs taken of the same scene. Brown continued to carry his sketch book to record his Vietnam war experience after college graduation, during his year and a half exploration of Central and South America after Vietnam, and over the eight years he lived in Guatemala, Central America.

Brown is an award-winning architect of health care and educational facilities for Native American communities from Montana, Idaho and South Dakota to Arizona and New Mexico. His pen and ink drawing skills propelled a colleague and him to create a highly successful training program, Field Drawing Academy, that is held in an outdoor environment. Brown's illustrations have been published in numerous books and magazines including Architectural Record.

Brown, a Fellow of the American Institute of Architects, is a former American Institute of Architects National Vice President and twice an American Institute of Architects Richard Upjohn Fellow. He is the only architect in the history of the American Institute of Architects to have won both the prestigious national American Institute of Architects Edward C. Kemper Award, for significant contributions to the profession, and the American Institute of Architects Whitney Young Jr. Award for his "dedication to serving his fellow humans and his profession with respect, integrity, dignity, and compassion."

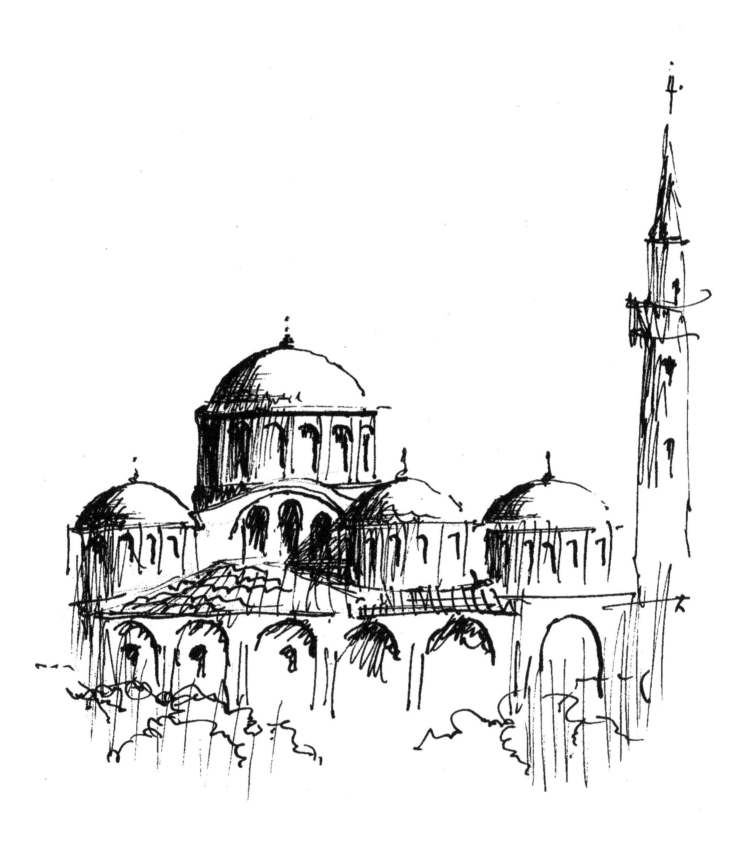

CPSIA information can be obtained
at www.ICGtesting.com
Printed in the USA
LVOW06s2251281217
561139LV00008B/10/P